Guide to Nuclear Weapons

Bradford Peace Studies Papers: New Series

No. 1 *In the Middle: Non-official Mediation in Violent Situations* Adam Curle

Bradford Peace Studies Papers: New Series No. 2

Guide to Nuclear Weapons

Paul Rogers

BERG
Oxford / New York / Hamburg
Distributed exclusively in the US and Canada by
ST. MARTIN'S PRESS, New York

Published in 1988 by
Berg Publishers Limited
77 Morrell Avenue, Oxford OX4 1NQ, UK
175 Fifth Avenue/Room 400, New York, NY 10010, USA
Schenefelder Landstr. 14K, 2000 Hamburg 55, FRG

British Cataloguing in Publication Data

Rogers, Paul.
Guide to nuclear weapons —
(Bradford peace studies papers. New series; No. 2).
1. Nuclear weapons
I. Title II. Series
355.8′25119 U264

ISBN 0–85496–150–X

Library of Congress Cataloging-in-Publication Data

Rogers, Paul.
Guide to nuclear weapons/Paul Rogers.
p. cm. — (Bradford peace studies papers; new ser., no. 2)
Bibliography: p.
Includes index.
ISBN 0–85496–150–X
1. Nuclear weapons. I. Title. II. Series.
U264.R65 1987
355.8′25119—dc 19 87–21711

Printed in Great Britain by Billings of Worcester

Contents

Tables

Acknowledgements

In the School of Peace Studies, Malcolm Dando, Malcolm Chalmers, Owen Greene, Shaun Gregory, Andrew Kelly, Pat Litherland, Peter Southwood, Steve Schofield and James O'Connell were all helpful with the collection of information. Lee Chadwick, Dan Plesch, Scilla McLean and Malcolm Spaven were all valued external sources.

Paul Rogers

Abbreviations

ABM	Anti-ballistic Missile
ACA	Advanced Combat Aircraft
ACM	Advanced Cruise Missile
ADM	Atomic Demolition Munition
AFAP	Artillery-fired Atomic Projectile
AFSATCOM	Air Force Satellite Communications
AIRS	Advanced Inertial Reference Sphere
ALCM	Air-launched Cruise Missile
AMaRV	Advanced Maneouvrable Re-entry Vehicle
ASAT	Anti-satellite Weapon
ASLV	Augmented Satellite Launch Vehicle
ASMP	*Air-sol à moyenne portée*
ASROC	Anti-submarine Rocket
ASW	Anti-submarine Warfare
ATACMS	Army Tactical Missile System
ATB	Advanced Technology Bomber
ATF	Advanced Tactical Fighter
ATH	Autonomous Terminal Homing
AWRE	Atomic Weapons Research Establishment
BAOR	British Army of the Rhine
BMD	Ballistic Missile Defence
CEP	Circular Error Probable
CERN	Controller of R & D Establishment, Research and Nuclear
CSRL	Common Strategic Rotary Launcher
DARPA	Defence Advanced Research Projects Agency
DISMAC	Digital Scene-matching Area Correlation
DoD	Department of Defense
ECM	Electronic Counter-measures
EFA	European Fighter Aircraft
EPW	Earth Penetrating Warhead
ERW	Enhanced Radiation (Neutron) Warhead
FGA	Fighter, Ground Attack
FROG	Free Rocket Over Ground
GLCM	Ground-launched Cruise Missile
GSFG	Group of Soviet Forces in Germany
IAEA	International Atomic Energy Agency
ICBM	Intercontinental Ballistic Missile
ICCM	Intercontinental Cruise Missile

INF	Intermediate Nuclear Force
IOC	Initial Operational Capability
IRBM	Intermediate-range Ballistic Missile
LTV	Ling-Temco-Vought
MAD	Magnetic Anomaly Detector
MaRV	Maneouvrable Re-entry Vehicle
MASM	Modular Air-to-surface Missile
MIRV	Multiple Independently targetable Re-entry Vehicle
MLRS	Multiple Launch Rocket System
MR	Maritime Reconnaissance
MRBM	Medium-range Ballistic Missile
MRV	Multiple Re-entry Vehicle
MSBS	*Mer-sol balistique stratégique*
MSOW	Modular Stand-off Weapon
NBC	Nuclear, Biological, Chemical
PSLV	Polar Satellite Launch Vehicle
RADAG	Radar Area Guidance
RV	Re-entry Vehicle
SAC	Strategic Air Command
SADM	Small Atomic Demolition Munition
SDI	Strategic Defense Initiative
SICBM	Small Intercontinental Ballistic Missile
SIPRI	Stockholm International Peace Research Institute
SLBM	Submarine-launched Ballistic Missile
SLCM	Submarine-launched Cruise Missile
SRAM	Short-range Attack Missile
SRINF	Shorter-range Intermediate Nuclear Force
SSB	Ship, Submersible, Ballistic
SSBN	Ship, Submersible, Ballistic, Nuclear
SSBS	*Sol-sol balistique stratégique*
SSN	Ship, Submersible, Nuclear
STOVL	Short Take-off, Vertical Landing
TAV	Transatmospheric Hypervelocity Vehicle
TEL	Transporter-erector-launcher
TERCOM	Terrain Contour Matching
UCOR	Uranium Enrichment Corporation (of South Africa)
VRBM	Variable-range Ballistic Missile

Overview

When the last edition of this guide was published in 1984, the review section made the point that there had, in the previous forty years, been periods of intense expansion of nuclear arsenals, but it concluded that the mid-1980s represented a period of remarkable acceleration by any previous standards. The evidence showed that

> an across-the-board process of quantitative *and* qualitative expansion of nuclear weapons is taking place in the mid-1980s and is likely to continue for some years to come. This involves the strategic, intermediate and tactical nuclear weapons of the superpowers as well as the nuclear arsenals of the smaller nuclear powers. It is not an exaggeration to describe this as a new nuclear arms race. It is a process which makes nonsense of a supposed commitment to arms control.*

In the late 1980s there appears, superficially, to have been a change. We would appear to be in a period of intense negotiation on arms control which involves discussions on strategic and intermediate nuclear weapons and on space-based systems. A 'zero option' agreement concerning intermediate nuclear forces in Europe appears probable, and discussions on major limits to strategic arsenals continue.

The evidence from this guide, however, is that the development and production of new weapons is proceeding entirely unaffected by these negotiations. In 1984 systems such as the M–X Peacekeeper and SS–25 ICBMs, the SS–N–23 SLBM and the B–1B strategic bombers were still being developed. Now they are being deployed. Projects such as the Advanced Cruise Missile, the Advanced Technology Bomber and the Blackjack were only talked about in rather vague terms. Now all are being flight-tested and there seems no doubt that they will shortly enter service.

The M–X Peacekeeper entered service in December 1986, just two months after the first squadron of B–1B bombers were

***Guide to Nuclear Weapons 1984–85*, Bradford University, 1984.

deployed. The SS–25 was first deployed a few months before that, and by the end of 1986 2 *Delta IV* submarines carrying SS–N–23 missiles had been commissioned. The Advanced Technology Bomber is now known as the B–2 and will enter service within four years. Already the next generation of long-range strike aircraft is being researched, as are even more advanced forms of cruise missile.

As discussed in the last edition, it is not just the increase in numbers which is significant; even more so is the qualitative enhancement. Central to this has been the steady increase in ballistic missile accuracy, enabling strategic counter-force weapons to be deployed at an accelerating rate. In the mid-1980s, the weapons in this category were on the fringe of effective counter-force capability. The Minuteman III and the Mod 4 version of the SS–18 each had accuracies of rather better than 1,000 feet CEP. Now, however, missiles are being deployed which are dramatic improvements on that, the Peacekeeper having a CEP of around 400 feet.

Even now, these missiles are being deployed in small numbers, but within four years this will change drastically. As the Trident D5 comes into service with the United States and improved versions of the SS–18 and SS–24 are fielded by the Soviet Union, some thousands of counter-force strategic missile warheads will be deployed by the early 1990s. This will cause formidable problems for crisis stability and will greatly accelerate the trend towards strategic nuclear war-fighting.

Two other trends may be discerned from the present record of nuclear weapons developments. One was apparent in the 1984 edition — the widespread commitment to small air-breathing cruise missiles. The ground-launched cruise missiles in Western Europe which have caused so much political controversy are just one small part of this. They would total 464 if fully deployed. By comparison, the US Navy is acquiring 758 nuclear-armed sea-launched cruise missiles and the US Air Force has already deployed around 1,700 air-launched missiles. A similar number of the Advanced Cruise Missile will be built, giving a total deployment of over 4,500 cruise missiles by the early 1990s.

The Soviet Union has already deployed several hundred air-launched cruise missiles and has a number of ground- and sea-launched systems under development. Many of these, and their US equivalents, will be deployed in dual-capable form, making problems of verification in the event of arms control agreements acutely difficult.

The second trend concerns developments in nuclear warhead technology. Stimulated partly by the financing of strategic defence research and partly by the requirement to enhance counter-force capabilities, a wide range of new warhead types is under development. One broad category concerns warheads designed specifically for destroying hardened underground targets such as missile silos or command bunkers. These earth penetrating warheads require a remarkable resistance to decceleration coupled with extreme accuracy of delivery. Given these possibilities, they can then be designed with relatively small yields and consequent low levels of collateral effects. This, in turn, results in their being unlikely to cause major atmospheric disruptions such as 'nuclear winter' effects. They are therefore highly suited to strategic nuclear war-fighting.

A second category of warhead developments is the third generation of warheads. These are devices which either release their energy in particular forms, such as intense neutron bursts or electromagnetic pulses, or else they are directional in effect. Many of the directional-warhead developments are closely related to research on strategic defence, and involve low yield devices intended for detonation above the atmosphere. The technology being developed, however, is likely to have very much wider implications — directional-effect warheads would achieve targeting accuracies of a very high order with low levels of collateral damage. They would thus tend to be far more militarily useable than current nuclear weapons.

At the more general level, arms control negotiations are shown by this study to be paralleled by a continuing enhancement in the quality and quantity of nuclear weapons, especially at the strategic level. Prospects for arms control at the intermediate level may look good, but it is already apparent that a variety of devices is available to be employed to bypass any treaty. Thus a removal of cruise, Pershing 2 and SS–20 missiles would leave a perceived targeting gap which could readily be filled by sea- and air-launched cruise missiles and depressed trajectory SLBMs.

At the strategic level, there are suggestions of a series of major cuts in strategic warheads. Whether this is feasible, given the momentum of the new programmes, is debatable. Of more concern is the reality that progress in this area could be seriously counterproductive. Thus a 50 per cent reduction in strategic warheads, if it resulted in smaller arsenals of counter-force warheads, would be considerably less stable than even the existing situation. Because of

their first-strike capabilities, these arsenals could be employed far more readily than those presently available.

What is actually required as the major priority is a freeze on new deployments of strategic weapons, followed by progressive removal of existing systems. Unless this is achieved we would face the paradox of nuclear disarmament producing an increasingly unstable strategic environment. The first step towards a freeze is a comprehensive test ban, but this now seems far in the future. It must therefore be assumed that genuine progress towards a more stable strategic environment is unlikely.

The major conclusion of this documentation of nuclear arsenals is that their expansion and enhancement is continuing as if arms control negotiations do not exist. If as much attention was paid to the weapons developments as to the negotiations, then our current predicament might be more widely recognised.

United States

The expanding defence budgets of the early 1980s brought in by the first and second Reagan administrations resulted, by the mid-1980s, in a marked expansion of US nuclear forces, especially at the strategic level. These included the M–X Peacekeeper ICBM, the Air-launched Cruise Missile, the B–1B strategic bomber and the *Ohio*-class ballistic missile submarine. A further effect was the development of new strategic weapons such as the 'Midgetman' SICBM, the Advanced Cruise Missile, the B–2 Advanced Technology Bomber and the advanced Trident D5 SLBM. At the intermediate and tactical levels, deployment of the ground- and sea- launched cruise missiles, the Pershing 2, enhanced radiation (neutron) warheads and modernised artillery all commenced during the mid-1980s, although a number of obsolete systems were withdrawn from service.

The other notable feature of the mid-1980s was the intense research and development activity concerned with advanced nuclear warheads. Part of the impetus came from the Strategic Defense Initiative, but this was combined with a perceived need to be able to target and destroy heavily hardened command facilities and mobile missiles. Third-generation directional nuclear warheads and earth penetrating warheads were among the programmes which, by 1985, were causing considerable excitement among the weapons designers at Los Alamos and Lawrence Livermore laboratories.

Intercontinental Ballistic Missiles

The ICBM leg of the US strategic triad is the least important in terms of numbers of warheads, less than 20 per cent of US strategic warheads being carried on ICBMs. Even so, the force is important in terms of accuracy, readiness, reliability and targeting flexibility, and is being enhanced by the production and deployment of the

M–X Peacekeeper missile. The existing Minuteman force is subject to continual improvements and a new missile, the so-called 'Midgetman' SICBM is under development.

Titan II LGM–25C

This was the largest missile in the US strategic inventory and was first deployed in 1963, carrying a 9-megaton W53 thermonuclear warhead on a General Electric Mark 6 re-entry vehicle. The liquid-fuelled missile was unreliable and the whole force was progressively withdrawn from service between 1983 and early 1987. Some of the missiles are likely to be converted to space launch vehicles.

Minuteman II LGM 30F

This missile is essentially an improved version of the Minuteman I ICBM and was built by Boeing, entering service in 1966. It is silo-based at sites in Montana, Missouri and Utah and is a 3-stage solid-fuel missile with a launch-weight of 31 tons. It has a range of 7,000 miles carrying a Mark 11 re-entry vehicle equipped with a W56 thermonuclear warhead variously rated at between 1.2 and 1.5 megatons. Missiles in service number 450, although 8 are equipped with the Emergency Rocket Communications System rather than a warhead. This is designed to provide emergency pre-launch communications facilities for US strategic forces, should satellite communications be destroyed by Soviet ASAT systems in wartime.

The on-board computer can store coordinates for up to 8 targets but retargeting with new coordinates is very slow, possibly taking 36 hours. During 1985, approximately two-thirds of the Minuteman II force were retrofitted with the Minuteman III command data buffer system to permit rapid retargeting (see following entry). Minuteman II accuracy is of the order of 1,200 feet CEP. Although it is an old missile, the Minuteman II is regarded as highly reliable. In early 1987 it was reported that both Minuteman II and III missiles and their launch facilities were undergoing the Rivet Mile maintenance refurbishment to prevent long-term deterioration. It was expected that both missiles could remain operational until the end of the century.

Minuteman III LGM 30G

This more advanced version of the Minuteman II was in production from 1970 to 1978, and 550 are deployed at bases in Montana, Wyoming and North Dakota, 50 of them being replaced by the M–X Peacekeeper over the period from 1986 to 1988. Another 100 missiles are in store and some could theoretically be fired from silos at Vandenburg Air Force Base (AFB) in California, although the hot-launch technique means that silos can only be used once. The Minuteman III has a launch-weight of 34 tons and a range of 8,000 miles.* The W62 170-kiloton warhead is carried in the Mark 12 re-entry vehicles of 250 of the missiles (declining to 200). Fitted with the NS–20 guidance system these have an accuracy of 840 feet CEP. The remaining 300 missiles, with a similar guidance system, carry the Mark 12A re-entry vehicle fitted with a W78 warhead rated at 335 kilotons. This combination gives an accuracy of 600 feet CEP. Both systems are 3-MIRV and the more advanced system was the world's most effective MIRVed hard-target ICBM prior to M–X deployment in 1986.

The Minuteman III force is fitted with the command data buffer system which permits individual missile retargetting in 25 minutes with each missile being able to be aimed at 3 targets as a norm. Retargeting of the entire force can be completed in 10 hours. As with the Minuteman II force, the missiles and their control systems are being continually updated, a recently completed programme involving a hardening of the silos to 2,000 p.s.i.

M–X Peacekeeper LGM–118A

The Peacekeeper is the main ICBM currently being produced by the United States, although the original plans for 200 missiles are unlikely to be fulfilled. The prime contractor is Martin Marietta and the missile is 71 feet long, weighs 68 tons and has a throw- weight of just under 8,000 lb, over 3 times that of the Minuteman III. The Peacekeeper is a 4-stage missile, the first 3 stages being solid fuelled and the final, post-boost stage using a storable liquid propellant. Range is about 8,000 miles and the Advanced Inertial Reference Sphere guidance package gives a CEP variously reported to be 300

*Speed at burn-out is around 15,000 m.p.h. and the highest point on the trajectory is around 700 miles.

to 400 feet, making the Peacekeeper by far the most accurate long-range ballistic missile currently operational.

The Peacekeeper can carry 12 warheads but is currently fitted with 10 W87 warheads, each carried in a Mark 21 re-entry vehicle. The W87 is similar to the 335-kiloton W78 warhead fitted to the modified Minuteman III ICBM, but is reported to have a variable yield of up to 475 kilotons. It appears that the normal yield is currently set at 300 kilotons. It is likely that the Peacekeeper will eventually be retrofitted with some kind of precision guided re-entry vehicle with the manoeuvrability allowing precise targeting and BMD avoidance. Terminal guidance could involve radar or laser sensing and could give CEPs of below 100 feet. A related development would be the fitting of earth penetrating warheads for use against underground hard targets.

Following a troubled passage through Congress, the financing of the Peacekeeper programme was initially limited to 50 missiles, funding for a further 50 missiles being dependent on the development of a survivable basing mode. Between Fiscal Years (FYs) 1984 and 1987 66 missiles were funded, but many were for test purposes. The first of 20 tests took place from Vandenburg over the Pacific Test Range on 17 June 1983, and the sixteenth test was conducted on 16 February 1987. Of these 16 tests, all but one were judged fully successful and one was partially successful, an unusually high success rate for a completely new missile.

The first 10 Peacekeeper missiles were installed in modified Minuteman III silos at the F E Warren Air Force Base in Wyoming in the latter part of 1986 and were declared operational on 22 December. Twenty-seven were operational by September 1987 and the full 50 will be by the end of 1988. The Peacekeeper uses a cold-launch technique involving gas-fired ejection from the silo with main-stage ignition when the missile is more than 50 feet above the silo. Burn-time, at 150 seconds, is the shortest for any operational missile.

A wide variety of basing modes was suggested for the Peacekeeper during the early 1980s, but by the end of 1986 a rail-mobile form had been selected and had gained considerable support in the DoD and Congress. This system will involve 25 trains each carrying 2 missiles in transporter-erector-launchers disguised as ordinary railcars. Each train will also have a launch-control car and 2 security waggons and all 25 trains will be able to move freely about the US rail network, some 200,000 miles of track. The F E Warren AFB has been chosen

as the initial location, but the USAF has identified 10 further possible bases in 8 states throughout the United States. Of the 50 missiles planned for this basing mode, the Reagan administration is seeking 21 in FY 1988 and 21 in FY 1989, the presumption being that an IOC could be achieved by 1991.

Thus the planned deployment of Peacekeeper ICBMs would be 100 missiles, 50 in each basing mode. The USAF still seeks 200 missiles, alhough the increased importance attached to the Small ICBM (SICBM) now makes that an unlikely target. Even so, 1,000 warheads capable of destroying time-urgent hardened targets are a considerable addition to US strategic nuclear forces.

Small ICBM ('Midgetman')

The SICBM concept was promoted by Boeing in 1981 as one solution to the problem of increasing vulnerability of silo-based ICBMs. The idea was to produce a small long-range missile which could be carried on a hardened mobile launcher with some cross-country ability. The concept appeared to have been rejected in favour of a large deployment of the Peacekeeper, but increasing congressional problems with that programme lead to a reawakening of interest in the SICBM.

By mid-1985 the main contract had been awarded to Martin Marietta, although Boeing remained heavily involved and was selected to build the 14-wheeled all-terrain hardened mobile launcher. A number of launch-weight and warhead options have been considered, ranging up to a Minuteman III-type missile carrying a 3-MIRV system. Early missiles are more likely to carry a single warhead, probably a modification of the W87 with a yield of up to 500 kilotons. Northrop is developing a lightweight version of the AIRS guidance system used in the Peacekeeper and accuracy is expected to equal early versions of the Peacekeeper. The SICBM will have a length of 53 feet, a diameter of just under 4 feet and a launch-weight of 17 tons. The warhead will be carried in a Mark 21 re-entry vehicle by Avco and the missile will also carry penetration aids. Range will be about 6,000 miles. Advanced guidance systems, including ring laser gyroscopes and stellar updates, are under development. The missile has 3 solid-fuel stages.

The SICBM will begin its flight-test programme in the winter of 1988/9 and an IOC of December 1992 is currently planned. A static firing test of a first-stage motor was completed by Morton Thiokol in

May 1987. Second and third stages will be by Aerojet and Hercules respectively.

Up to 500 SICBMs will be deployed, the initial base being Malstrom AFB, Montana, with later bases including Warren, Ellsworth and Holloman air force bases and possibly the Yuma Proving Grounds. Prime requirements are for large areas of military reservations for deploying the hardened mobile launchers, each of which will be designed to withstand a 20 p.s.i. overpressure, although the launchers will also use public roads. At Malstrom it is envisaged that launchers will be deployed in hardened shelters, 2 shelters being located adjacent to each existing Minuteman III silo. Between 150 and 250 SICBMs will be based at Malstrom. Each launch vehicle will have a single crew member who will drive the vehicle and place it in launch position. Launch procedures will be conducted remotely, with a single launch control centre being responsible for the force although it will be backed up by an airborne launch control system similar to that used for Minuteman III and Peacekeeper ICBMs. The SICBMs will also be backed up by several mobile ground control units also capable of launching missiles.

Advanced Strategic Missile Systems

Although no new ICBMs are currently planned after the Peacekeeper and SICBM deployments, a wide range of programmes is under way which collectively involve substantial improvements to existing missiles. A number of the technologies involved could also be applied to submarine-launched ballistic missiles such as Trident D5 and also air-launched stand-off missiles. There are four main areas of development, outlined below:

— *Manoeuvrable Re-entry Vehicles (MaRVs).* Programmes include the navy's Mark 500 Evader system which uses moveable weights within a re-entry vehicle to provide changes in direction, and the USAF's AMaRV which employs aerodynamic fins. Both of these are R & D programmes which have been in progress for several years. Technology demonstration flight tests of MaRVs are planned for 1991. They are heavier than ordinary re-entry vehicles; a Peacekeeper ICBM, for example, could carry just 8 MaRVs instead of 10 or 12 MIRVs.

— *Improved Guidance.* A range of programmes is concerned with improving guidance to enable CEPs of less than 100 feet to be achieved. These include further improvements in inertial guidance, stellar and satellite mid-course updates and terminal guidance, the latter involving attempts to marry technologies already in use with much slower missiles, such as the Pershing 2, to high-velocity ICBMs and SLBMs.

— *Earth Penetrating Warheads.* A major area of innovation is the development of earth penetrating warheads, particularly effective against hardened underground targets. A warhead detonated at a depth of 65 feet has a yield effectiveness more than 25 times greater than an equivalent surface burst, but earth penetrating warheads have appeared to be more suitable in relation to relatively slow missiles such as air-launched cruise missiles. Intensive research at Los Alamos and Lawrence Livermore appears to have lead to the belief that fast missile EPWs are now feasible, and the DoD was reported, in June 1987, to be commencing a major project study.

— *Targeting Mobile Systems.* An area of intense current research is the targeting of mobile missiles. While much of the work is concerned with using penetrating bombers and smart stand-off weapons, it is also believed that fast strategic missiles have a role. Target acquisition by remote sensing followed by missile mid-course updates could be accompanied by specialised ICBM or SLBM warheads for use against mobile ICBMs which include the so-called 'electronic kill' warhead designed to yield intense electromagnetic pulse effects to disable mobile ICBM electronics.

The aim of this mix of technologies would be to produce, by the mid-1990s, advanced versions of the Peacekeeper, SICBM and Trident D5 which can survive a hostile BMD environment, achieve accuracies of at least 100 feet CEP and carry warheads tailored for specific tasks such as hard-target destruction and targeting of mobile systems. By the end of the 1990s the United States could expect to have over 6,000 time-urgent strategic warheads for such functions.

Submarine-launched Ballistic Missiles

Although the US SLBM force is substantially smaller than that of the Soviet Union, both in terms of the number of submarines and the number of missiles, all of the missiles are MIRVed with 8- or 10-MIRV systems. As a result, the warhead total is far higher than that of the Soviet Union. The most significant current development is the Trident D5 missile, which will enter service in 1989 with an accuracy sufficient to make it the world's first SLBM with hard-target potential.

The US Navy has recently invested heavily in attempts to improve communications with submarines at sea. An extremely low-frequency radio communications system has recently been completed involving 84 miles of antenna on 2 sites 170 miles apart in Michigan and Wisconsin. Satellite-based communications systems, including a scanning blue-green laser, are also being investigated.

Poseidon C3 UGM–73A

The Poseidon SLBM is built by Lockheed and was first test- fired in 1970, becoming operational in March 1971. It is a 2-stage solid-fuel missile weighing 29 tons and is 34 feet in length. It has a range of 2,500 miles and carries the Mark 3 MIRV system with 6 to 14 re-entry vehicles. Each carries a 400 lb W68 warhead rated at 40 kilotons and has a CEP of 1,500 feet. The 2,500 mile range is for a 10-MIRV assembly and increases with fewer warheads. The 10-MIRV assembly is the standard configuration although some Poseidon SLBMs are reported to carry 14-MIRV systems with a reduced range.

The Poseidon missile is carried on 6 *Franklin-*, 2 *Madison-* and 8 *Lafayette-*class SSBN, making 16 boats in all. Each boat has 16 vertical launch tubes, so that 256 missiles are currently deployed. In 1985 and 1986 3 Poseidon boats were withdrawn from service to comply with SALT II limits, but this practice ceased in late 1986. It is likely that the 16 remaining boats will be maintained in service until the mid-1990s.

Poseidon submarines are the only US strategic systems which have an overseas base. Seven boats normally operate from Holy Loch in Scotland, the facility consisting of missile submarine tender, a floating dock and support ships. The tender can service 3 SSBN simultaneously and carries up to 20 spare missiles and conventional

ordinance. Until early 1987, the tender at Holy Loch was the USS *Hunley*, but it was replaced, in June 1987, by the USS *Simon Lake*, a tender which has been modified to support Trident C4 missiles. This may mean that such missiles will be deployed on submarines operating from Holy Loch.

Trident C4 UGM–93A

Also known as the Trident I, this is the third generation of SLBMs to be produced by Lockheed. It is similar in size but slightly heavier than the Poseidon and carries a similar throw-weight over a much longer range — of the order of 4,600 miles. Trident C4 can carry 10 re-entry vehicles but is normally equipped with just 8 in a MIRV system. Mark 4 re-entry vehicles are used which carry the W76 warhead rated at 100 kilotons. Over the period 1978 to 1982 12 missile submarines previously equipped with Poseidon SLBMs were retrofitted with the Trident C4 missile. The missile is also carried on 8 *Ohio*-class submarines which will eventually be retrofitted with the much more advanced Trident D5.

The *Ohio*-class SSBN is the world's most heavily armed SSBN although it is smaller than the Soviet *Typhoon* class. It has a length of 560 feet, a displacement of 18,700 tons and carries 24 missiles in vertical launch tubes. They are constructed at the Groton, Connecticut shipyard of the Electric Boat Division of General Electric and the first boat, the USS *Ohio*, entered service in November 1981. Originally planned at 15, construction of this class rose to 20 and, more recently, 23, with production planned at one a year to the end of the century. Table 1 (over) gives a provisional list of submarines and their dates of commission.

Over the period 1988 to 1992 5 more submarines will be ordered. The *Pennsylvania* will be commissioned late in 1989 and will carry the Trident D5 missile as will all subsequent submarines in the class. The first 8 boats will eventually be retrofitted with the D5 missile. Until the mid-1990s, the number of Trident C4 missiles in service will be 384 with 3,072 warheads.

Trident D5

The name implies that this is an improvement of the Trident C4, but it is actually an entirely new missile, substantially larger than the C4 and very much more accurate. Full-scale development commenced

Table 1 US USSBN and their dates of commission

Designation	Class	Year
SSBN 726	*Ohio*	1981
SSBN 727	*Michigan*	1982
SSBN 728	*Florida*	1983
SSBN 729	*Georgia*	1984
SSBN 730	*Henry L. Jackson*	1984
SSBN 731	*Alabama*	1985
SSBN 732	*Alaska*	1986
SSBN 733	*Nevada*	1986
SSBN 734	*Tennessee*	1988
SSBN 735	*Pennsylvania*	1989
SSBN 736	—	1990
SSBN 737	—	1991
SSBN 738	—	1992
SSBN 739	—	1993

in 1982 and test-flights started in 1987. The 44-foot-long missile weighs over 55 tons and has a range in excess of 4,000 miles depending on the payload. Throw-weight is double that of Trident C4 and the 3-stage solid-fuelled missile has a total burn-time of 170 seconds. It carries the Mark 5 re-entry vehicle, a version of the Mark 21 RV used in the Peacekeeper ICBM, and each missile can carry up to 15 MIRVs, although one report suggests 17. The missile employs the Mark 6 inertial-guidance systems which utilises stellar update and is expected to give an accuracy of 400 feet CEP, conferring on the missile considerable hard-target capabilities.

Trident D5 is expected to be fitted initially with the W87 variable-yield strategic warhead. At least 312 missiles will be deployed by 1998, but the final total may be much higher. Even at that level, the addition of around 4,000 highly accurate warheads to the US strategic inventory will be highly significant. IOC is late 1989.

Further SLBM Developments

The decision to continue production of *Ohio*-class boats throughout the 1990s suggests that earlier plans to develop a smaller SSBN and possibly a new SLBM have been shelved. However, as the Poseidon boats are withdrawn from service during the mid-1990s, the entire SLBM force of the United States will be deployed on around 20 vessels. Many analysts argue that this is too few and advocate a

further SSBN/SLBM programme, and the Navy Secretary's Office has spoken of maintaining a fleet of 40 SSBN in the mid- and late 1990s. Because of the high cost of Trident D5 and its associated submarines, it is probable that a further programme will evolve by 1995 involving a new smaller class of SSBN.

Long-range Bombers and Associated Missiles

The United States has long placed heavy reliance on its force of strategic bombers, and a succession of intercontinental bombers has been maintained commencing with the B–36 and progressing through the B–52, the B–58, the B–1B and, in the near future, the B–2. Aerial refuelling has enabled shorter-range bombers to maintain an intercontinental ability and the FB–111A remains in service with such back-up. The common pattern is for the most modern bomber to be allocated the penetration bombing role and older planes to perform a stand-off function, armed with appropriate missiles. There is currently an extensive programme of bomber and missile developments.

Boeing B–52 Stratofortress

Nearly 750 of this large 8-engined long-range subsonic bomber were built between 1954 and 1962, the planes forming the backbone of the Strategic Air Command forces in the 1960s, being deployed in the strategic penetration role with large thermonuclear bombs such as the 9-megaton B53. The latest models of the B–52, the B–52G and B–52H will remain in service until the latter end of the 1990s, and all have undergone considerable refurbishment and upgrading. The B–52 has a maximum take-off weight of nearly 220 tons and a range of 7,500 miles at a ceiling of 55,000 feet. Although B–52s now in service are available for conventional roles such as maritime strike and land attack, their prime role is that of the strategic nuclear bomber. In this role, they are handing over the penetration role to the B–1B and are retaining the stand-off role for which they are equipped with Short-Range Attack Missiles and Air-Launched Cruise Missiles.

The B–52G can carry 8 SRAMs internally and 12 ALCMs on underwing pylons. The B–52H is being modified with the Common Strategic Rotary Launcher (CSRL) which can enable it to carry a

mix of SRAMs and ALCMs internally. The first CSRL-equipped B–52H should be fully operational with SAC by mid-1988 and all such planes will be retrofitted with the CSRL by August 1993. The CSRL can also take nuclear and conventional bombs.

As the B–52 fleet assumes the stand-off role, they are being deployed with the ALCM, a process which started in 1982. By early 1987, 136 B–52s had been retrofitted with ALCMs, the SALT II limit of 130 having been passed on 28 November 1986. B–52s are being modified at the rate of one every three weeks through to early 1990, with an eventual deployment of 194 ALCM-fitted B–52s. The remaining 61 B–52s have been assigned to conventional roles.

FB–111A

With the failure of the B–58A Hustler to fulfil its early expectations as a supersonic strategic bomber, the F–111 was upgraded to the strategic FB–111A, being supported in such a role by tanker aircraft. Between 1966 and 1971 76 FB–111As were built, and 55 remain in service. It is a 2-seat, twin-engine, supersonic all-weather low-level penetration bomber with an unrefuelled range of 3,400 miles. It can carry 2 SRAMs or nuclear bombs in its internal bomb bay at supersonic speeds, and 4 more in underwing pylons, although this limits performance. It is normally deployed with the B43 or B61 bombs as alternatives to SRAMs. The FB–111A is currently assigned to Strategic Air Command whereas the shorter-range F–111s are deployed with Tactical Air Command, principally in Europe. They are described under the heading of Intermediate Nuclear Forces.

B–1B

The B–1B strategic bomber programme is one of the longest-lived in aviation history, having been developed originally in the early 1970s as a long-term replacement for the B–58 and B–52. It was cancelled in 1977 although funds were allocated to keep prototypes flying, and the programme was reactivated when the Reagan Administration came to power in 1981.

Extensive further developments and improvements were undertaken and the plane was designated the B–1B. The B–1B is a variable geometry 4-jet supersonic penetration and stand-off bomber with a crew of 4, a maximum take-off weight of some 215 tons and a

range in excess of 8,000 miles. In the low-level penetration role it is subsonic and flies at 50 to 300 feet using forward-looking and terrain-following radar backed up by an advanced inertial navigation system and an AFSATCOM satellite navigation link.

It has 3 internal weapons bays and 2 sets of underwing pylons. Internally it can carry 8 ACMs, 24 SRAMs, 12 B28s or 24 B61/83 nuclear bombs. Externally it can carry 14 ACMs/SRAMs, 8 B28s or 14 B43/61/83s. Its maximum nuclear weapons loading is thus 38. The B–1B could be fitted with the ALCM but it is more likely that the ALCM deployments will be restricted to the B–52 whereas the B–1B will receive the ACM.

Delivery of B–1Bs to Strategic Air Command commenced in July 1985, and the first squadron reached its IOC at Dyess Air Force Base, Texas, on 1 October 1986. Construction of 100 planes is scheduled although there could be an attrition buy of perhaps 10 more. The deployment of the B–1B should be completed by the end of 1988 at the following bases:

Dyess AFB, Texas	29
Ellsworth AFB, South Dakota	35
Grand Forks AFB, North Dakota	17
McConnell AFB, Kansas	17

Deployment of B–1Bs to Dyess was completed by early 1987, deployment to Ellsworth commenced at the end of January, and to Grand Forks towards the end of the year.

The B–1B uses a variety of stealth anti-radar technologies, including surface design and the use of non-radar-reflecting skins to cut the radar signature to one-thousandth of that of the B–52. Advocates of a more advanced B–1C or a further buy of B–1Bs were vocal in the mid-1980s, but the continued progress in the development of the B–2 precluded this.

B–2 (Advanced Technology Bomber)

The B–2 ATB, the so-called 'stealth' bomber, was first announced in 1980 but the programme has remained highly classified and few firm details of design and performance are available although the flight-test programme was due to start in early 1987. The B–2 is being produced by Northrop at its Palmdale plant some 75 miles north-east of Los Angeles. Six prototype and pre-production aircraft

are being built and the first of 132-production aircraft should enter service by 1992 at the Whiteman Air Force Base in Missouri. Each B–2 is expected to cost in excess of $300 million.

The B-2 is essentially a flying wing design with a take-off weight of around 170 tons and a weapons load of a little over 18 tons. This gives it a weapons load substantially less than that of the B–1B but the intention is to avoid dependence on aerial refuelling, so the B–2 should have a range well in excess of 8,000 miles. The plane is reported to be powered by 2 General Electric unreheated turbofans and to incorporate highly sophisticated anti-radar features.

The B–2 is to be deployed as a penetrating bomber designed to cruise at high altitude at subsonic speeds and to be effectively impervious to radar and infra-red detection. All offensive weapons will be carried internally and these may include the Advanced Cruise Missile as well as gravity nuclear bombs. A significant function of the B–2 will be a capability against relocatable targets such as mobile ICBMs.

As the B–2 enters service in large numbers during the 1990s, the B–1B will be deployed primarily as a stand-off bomber and the B–52 will revert to a conventional role with the majority being withdrawn by the end of the decade.

Transatmospheric Hypersonic Vehicle X–30A (TAV)

The TAV programme was announced in February 1986 with considerable publicity and some emphasis on civil applications in the form of the 'Orient Express' civil airliner. By late 1986, almost all aspects of the programme had become highly classified, as the military aspects of the programme (80 per cent of project costs) began to dominate. The TAV is a hybrid aircraft/spacecraft designated the X–30A by the Department of Defense which will use conventional runways for take-off and landing but will be able to transfer to space and achieve speeds of Mach 25. Current plans call for the completion of 2 prototypes to fly by 1993 and a three-year $600 million research and development programme has been funded.

The X–30A may not itself develop into a military strike aircraft but it is likely to provide a range of technologies appropriate to a successor to the B–2.

Tanker Support

Although the B–2 is not intended to operate with tanker support, the FB–111A, B–52 and B–1B bombers all utilise aerial refuelling. The United States has by far the largest fleet of tanker aircraft including 615 KC–135s, a modification of the Boeing 707, and 48 of the much larger KC-10A, based on the McDonnell-Douglas DC–10. A further 10 KC–10As are on order.

Short-range Attack Missile (SRAM) AGM–69A

The Boeing SRAM, which entered service in 1972, was developed for defence suppression by penetrating bombers such as the B–52. The SRAM is 14 feet long, weighs 2,200 lb and can deliver a W69 170-kiloton thermonuclear warhead over a range varying from 50 to 140 miles depending on altitude, and at a speed of 2,000 m.p.h. The SRAM uses an inertial-guidance system together with a terrain clearance sensor. The B–52 can carry 8 SRAMs internally and 12 more on underwing pylons. The FB–111A can carry 6 SRAMs. By 1975 1,500 were procured to equip 17 B–52 wings and 2 FB–111A wings, and 1,175 remain in service, with just 120 of these assigned to the FB–111A wings. The SRAM will be augmented with and ultimately replaced by the SRAM II.

Short-range Attack Missile II (SRAM II)

SRAM II is being developed by Boeing as a more accurate and longer-range version of the SRAM. It will be about two-thirds of the size of the present missile but will carry a warhead of similar power, and will be deployed on the B–1B and B–2. Up to 20 SRAM II missiles will be carried internally in the B–1B. Although it will have a substantially longer range, the accuracy will be greatly improved. Planned CEP for the missile is not yet known but is intended to give it a capability for destroying hard targets. An earth penetrator warhead could be fitted.

SRAM II will be powered by a Hercules-Bacchus rocket-motor and guidance will be by Litton. The $2.4 billion programme calls for initial test-flights by mid-1989 and deployment of 1,633 missiles over the period from 1991 to 1994.

Air-launched Cruise Missile AGM–86B (ALCM)

The production run for the Boeing ALCM was closed in September 1986 after a run of 1,715 missiles. These have now been delivered to the USAF where they will eventually be deployed on 194 B–52 bombers. The ALCM has also been tested on the B–1B and may also be deployed with this aircraft pending delivery of stocks of the Advanced Cruise Missile (ACM).

The ALCM is just under 21 feet in length and has a launch-weight of 3,200 lb. It has a range of around 1,700 miles at 500 m.p.h. in a low-altitude flight profile. It is powered by a modified Williams F107 turbofan and is guided by an inertial package supplemented by the TERCOM (Terrain Contour Matching) system and related terminal-guidance packages. One of these under development, Autonomous Terminal Homing (ATH), allows terminal re-targeting. The ALCM carries a W80–1 variable-yield warhead with a 5- to 150-kiloton range. It is not deployed in a conventionally armed form.

Before launch from the carrying aircraft, the missile's engine outlet, wings and fins are retracted for compact storage, being extended in the first few seconds after launch. The B–52G carries 12 ALCMs on underwing pylons. The B-52H will also carry 8 internally on the Common Strategic Rotary Launcher. TERCOM guidance depends on satellite-based topography mapping of potential flight paths. It was revealed in November 1986 that targeting data was being prepared to enable cruise missiles to be used against targets in the Middle East.

Advanced Cruise Missile AGM–129A (ACM)

The USAF originally required over 3,000 ALCMs, but this aim was abandoned when it became possible to develop an entirely new cruise missile which would utilise stealth technology to make it highly resistant to in-flight detection by radar. The Convair Division of General Dynamics was selected to develop the ACM in April 1983. Although the IOC will be reached at the K I Sawyer Air Force Base in Michigan by 1989 or 1990, very little is known about the performance of the missile. Flight-testing has commenced and the ACM is powered by a Williams F112 turbofan. It is a subsonic missile with an accuracy at least as good as the ALCM (CEP under 100 feet) and it will be deployed initially with the W80–1 5- to

150-kiloton warhead. In addition to stealth features, the main advantages of the ACM are likely to be a greater targeting flexibility, especially with relocatable targets, and a longer range. A range in excess of 2,000 miles is likely, particularly advantageous to the older B–52H bombers on which it will be initially deployed. The ACM will also be carried by the B–1B. At least 1,500 ACMs will be deployed.

Hypersonic Cruise Missile

Research and development concerned with technologies applicable to hypersonic cruise missiles is under way by DARPA. This appears related to a new generation of high-speed air-breathing missiles which might be developed in the 1990s.

Intercontinental Cruise Missile

There were reports in the early 1980s that a supersonic intercontinental cruise missile was under consideration, and the Vought Corporation was reported to be engaged in some initial research for DARPA. In the late 1950s, the US briefly deployed the inaccurate Snark ICCM but it was quickly outdated by the early ICBMs. New technologies of propulsion and guidance would now make an ICCM feasible but current indications are that stand-off missiles launched from manned bombers are the favoured line of development.

Ballistic Missile Defences

The United States developed a pair of anti-ballistic missiles (ABMs), Spartan and Sprint, in the early 1970s. They combined to produce a layered defence, with ranges of 400 and 20 miles respectively, and each carried a nuclear warhead. The system was broadly similar to the Galosh upgrade currently being developed by the Soviet Union around Moscow but the US system was deployed for only a few months due to doubts about its technical capabilities.

The Strategic Defense Initiative involves a very wide variety of anti-missile technologies, most of which are beyond the scope of this study as they are not nuclear-armed. Even so, a number of nuclear warhead developments related to anti-ballistic missile systems are now being researched. These involve third-generation nuclear war-

heads which aim to produce a directional energy release on detonation. The best-known of these is the X-ray pumped laser, in which a small nuclear explosion powers intense bursts of X-rays to be directed at missile targets. This is one of a group of projects, another being the so-called Project Prometheus, in which a nuclear detonation is used to produce a directed stream of hypervelocity particles intended to destroy decoy warheads in space.

The eventual status of third-generation nuclear warheads within the Strategic Defense Initiative is not clear, and they may form a small component of complex systems. However, the SDI programme has helped to stimulate intense interest in third-generation warheads and they may well be developed for purposes quite other than strategic defence.

Intermediate Nuclear Forces

The development and deployment of ground-launched cruise missiles and the Pershing 2 missile in Western Europe in the mid-1980s occasioned intense public debate. While the Pershing 2 does represent a highly significant improvement in ballistic missile technology, especially in relation to guidance and accuracy, the GLCMs are little more than the tip of the iceberg of cruise missile deployments, the air- and sea-launched variants being far more significant.

Ground-launched Cruise Missile BGM–109G (GLCM)

The GLCM is a variant of the General Dynamics Convair Division's Tomahawk cruise missile developed in the early 1970s. It is broadly similar in range and speed to the ALCM but requires a rocket-booster for launch. It is 21 feet long, has a wingspan of 8 feet and a launch-weight of 3,250 lb including rocket-booster. Its range is around 1,600 miles although test-flights of 2,000 miles are reported. The guidance combines an inertial package with TERCOM and accuracy is reported to be as low as 70 feet CEP. Propulsion is by the Williams F107 turbojet and the W84 warhead, originally reported to be a 200-kiloton-yield weapon, is now listed as a variable-yield weapon with a wide range of 0.2 to 150 kilotons. This results in a highly flexible missile appropriate for NATO's policy of flexible response.

The GLCM is stored in a protective aluminium cannister with its wings, fins and engine inlets folded, and can be fuelled in advance

and stored for some months without maintenance. GLCMs are carried in large 16-ton wheeled launch vehicles, protected against small-arms fire and NBC environments. Each vehicle carries 4 missiles and the launch tubes are angled at 45° for launching. Units are organised in flights of 16 missiles in 4 launch vehicles accompanied by 2 launch control centres and around 15 supporting vehicles with 69 personnel. A flight is intended to be dispersed up to 100 miles from base in a convoy at 18 m.p.h. using public highways, although firing sites tend to be on military land. All vehicles can be air-transported in C–141 and C–5 aircraft.

The full deployment of GLCMs in Western Europe is scheduled to be 464 by early 1988. Table 2 below gives base locations and final deployments.

At each base, GLCMs are stored in large underground silos with direct launcher access. Each silo takes 1 flight and can withstand a direct hit from a 2,000 lb conventional bomb. Limited protection against nuclear attack is offered. One flight at each base is reported to be on rapid alert and can be fired from within the base confines.

USAF GLCM personnel are trained at the US Tactical Air Command's 868th Tactical Missile Training Squadron at Davis-Monthan Air Force Base in Arizona, in courses lasting up to twelve weeks. Some 4,200 people are being trained for the West European deployments, with a similar number of support personnel.

Table 2 Base locations and deployments of GLCMs in Western Europe

Country	Final deployment	Deployment by June 1987
United Kingdom		
Greenham Common	96	96
Molesworth	64	0
Italy		
Comiso (Sicily)	112	80
West Germany		
Wüschheim	96	16
Netherlands		
Woensdrecht	48	0
Belgium		
Florennes	48	16

If an INF agreement is reached, it is possible that GLCMs could be withdrawn from Western Europe. It has been reported that GLCMs could be readily converted into Sea-launched Cruise Missiles (SLCMs) although an agreement might require dismantling.

Pershing 1A

The Pershing 1A is a mobile ballistic missile armed with a W50 nuclear warhead with yield options of 60, 200 and 400 kilotons. The missile is carried on a Ford wheeled launch vehicle and 72 launchers are deployed with the West German Army, the warheads being held in US custody. The Pershing 1A was developed primarily by Martin Marietta and has a range of 460 miles at a speed of up to 5,000 m.p.h. and a CEP of 1,400 feet. Until 1986 it was reported that each launcher in West Germany had one reload, implying a deployment of 144 missiles. It appears that this has been reduced to 100 missiles. When the US Army's Pershing 1A missiles in West Germany were replaced with the Pershing 2, it was reported that a reduced-range version, the Pershing 1B, might be made available to the West German armed forces. This idea was dropped but the possibility of a Pershing 1B system being developed if Pershing 2 missiles are withdrawn under an arms control agreement remains (see opposite).

Pershing 2

Although the Pershing 2 is technically a development of the Pershing 1A it is effectively a new missile system, the improvements in range and especially accuracy making it a formidable advance over the earlier missile. The Pershing 2 is the only ballistic missile of over 1,000 miles range to have terminal guidance, the speed and accuracy making it a unique counter-force nuclear weapon.

The Pershing 2 is produced by Martin Marietta and is a 34-foot-long 2-stage solid-fuel missile with a launch-weight of 7 tons and a throw-weight of just over 1,000 lb. It was originally reported to have a range of 1,000 miles, insufficient to reach Moscow from West Germany, and many analysts thought this was a deliberate underestimate. This suspicion appeared to be confirmed when 6 Pershing 2 missiles were test-launched in a three-hour period at Cape Canaveral in March 1987 in an operational readiness demonstration and were fired successfully over an 800 to 1,200 mile range.

The boost phase guidance is inertial and can be referenced at base before field dispersal. Reaction time in the field is under one hour and launchers can reload. Pershing 2 is equipped with Goodyear RADAG radar area correlation terminal guidance. As the re-entry vehicle completes its trajectory towards the target, a radar facility in the nose-cone generates radar images of the target area, initially over an area of some 400 square miles around the target, and compares this with a reference map stored on the on-board computer. This then generates course corrections which are implemented through aerodynamic fins. Accuracy is better than 150 feet CEP.

The Pershing 2 carries the W85 variable-yield warhead with a range of 0.3 to 80 kilotons, this wide range of yields giving considerable targeting flexibility. The planned W86 earth penetrating warhead was cancelled in 1981 but renewed interest in such warheads could now lead to a system being developed.

There are 108 launchers deployed with 3 army battalions in West Germany at Neu Ulm, Neckars Ulm and Schwäbisch-Gmünd. Each battalion has 4 batteries and each battery has 9 launchers, 1 battery in each battalion being on quick reaction alert. Each battery of 9 launchers has 13 missiles, but the 4 extra missiles are described as operational readiness floats rather than reloads. Thus 156 Pershing 2 missiles are actually based in West Germany. In addition, unconfirmed reports suggest that up to 30 missiles may be deployed in operational condition at Fort Sill in the United States for rapid deployment overseas in time of crisis.

Pershing 1B

Following progress in arms control negotiations in 1986/7, it became possible that missiles with a range of over 600 miles might be withdrawn from Europe. US DoD officials have proposed that Pershing 2 missiles be redeployed without the first stage to provide a force of missiles of under 600 miles range. Changes to launchers and guidance systems would be required but would not be major. Indeed it has been reported that at least 15 test-flights with such a reduced-range version have already been made. Similarly, it would be possible to upgrade the Pershing 1B missile to Pershing 2 status.

Sea-launched Cruise Missile BGM–109A (SLCM)

A series of sea-launched cruise missiles based on the Tomahawk is being deployed by the US Navy on a wide range of surface ships and submarines. Most are conventionally armed but a substantial proportion are nuclear-tipped. There are three main types:

— *Tomahawk Land Attack Missile — Nuclear (TLAM–N) BGM–109A*. This is broadly similar to the GLCM and carries a W80–0 5- to 150-kiloton warhead over a range of 1,600 miles. The accuracy is reported to be less than that of the GLCM at around 900 feet CEP.

— *Tomahawk Land Attack Missile — Conventional (TLAM–C) BGM–109C*. This is a 700-mile-range land attack missile carrying a 1,000 lb conventional warhead. It uses inertial guidance and TERCOM together with DISMAC terminal guidance to give an accuracy of under 100 feet CEP. A variant, the BGM–109D, equipped with sub-munitions, is under development.

— *Tomahawk Anti-ship Missile (TASM) BGM–109B*. This is a 300-mile-range anti-ship missile, also with a 1,000 lb warhead and using a combination of inertial guidance and an active radar terminal-guidance system derived from the Harpoon missile.

The US Navy plans to procure 3,994 Tomahawk SLCMs from General Dynamics and McDonnell Douglas by 1994, of which 758 will be nuclear-armed. By the end of Fiscal Year 1987 928 of all three types had been bought, of which approximately 318 were nuclear-tipped.

SLCMs of the different types are externally indistinguishable so it will not be possible to determine if a SLCM-equipped ship is carrying nuclear-armed missiles. By 1994 198 ships and submarines will be fitted with SLCMs, the main classes being:

Submarines: *Permit*
Sturgeon
Los Angeles
Surface ships: *Iowa* battleships

California cruisers
Long Beach cruisers
Virginia cruisers
Ticonderoga cruisers
Burke destroyers
Spruance destroyers

The main form of mounting on surface ships has been quadruple armoured-box launchers, nuclear-armed deployments commencing in June 1984. The most common future mounting will be the 61-cell Mark 41 vertical launcher which will take SLCMs and other missiles such as the ASROC. It is likely that the most important deployment mode for nuclear-tipped SLCMs will be submarine, principally in *Los Angeles*-class boats. These have been deployed with 8 SLCMs as part of their normal complement of torpedoes and Harpoon anti-ship missiles. The SLCMs are fired in capsule form from conventional torpedo tubes but a 12-tube vertical launch system has been fitted to *Los Angeles*-class boats from SSN 719 onwards. The tubes are fitted outside the pressure hull, forward of the dome bulkhead, with the missiles being fired through watertight hatches in the casing. The first SSN to be equipped in this manner was the *Pittsburgh* which was commissioned on 23 Novemver 1985.

F–111

Although the F–111 is often classified as a fighter-bomber, and it does maintain an interceptor capability, its main function is as a theatre nuclear bomber. Of the 280 remaining in service, 156 are stationed at Lakenheath and Upper Heyford in the UK. The F–111 is a Mach 2.5 2-seater swing-wing bomber with a maximum range of 2,800 miles and capable of carrying 25,000 lb of ordnance. In its nuclear-armed form it can carry 3 free-fall nuclear bombs, including the B43, B57, B61 and B83. Although the F–111 first entered service in 1967, the more recent variants are regarded as highly effective strike aircraft. A number were modified to produce the EF–111A unarmed electronic warfare aircraft which accompany the strike aircraft on missions to counter defensive measures.

F–15E Strike Eagle

The Strike Eagle is a medium-range interdiction version of the F–15

interceptor, which entered service with the USAF in January 1987. It is a supersonic all-weather nuclear-capable strike aircraft which will augment and eventually replace the F–111 in the theatre nuclear role, especially in Europe. Its range is broadly similar to that of the F–111 and it can carry a 25,000 lb weapons load. The USAF seeks to purchase 392 F–15Es by 1994.

Army Tactical Nuclear Weapons

Honest John MGR–1B

This old unguided artillery missile is still in service with the armies of Greece and Turkey, warheads being maintained in US custody. It is being withdrawn from service by late 1988.

Nike-Hercules MIM–14

Around 500 of this 100-mile-range anti-aircraft missile were deployed with several NATO forces in Europe until the mid-1980s, warheads being maintained in US custody. It is being phased out, usually in favour of the conventionally-armed Patriot missile. All will have been withdrawn by late 1988.

Lance MGM–52C

This is a surface-to-surface guided artillery missile which can deliver a nuclear or conventional warhead over a distance of up to 80 miles with a CEP at maximum range of 1,200 feet. It is produced by the Vought Corporation and is normally carried on an M–752 tracked launcher made by the Farm Machinery Corporation with another vehicle carrying 2 reloads and a loading hoist. The launch system allows rapid reloading with 15 minutes between firing. Lance has been in service since 1973 and carries the W70–1 or W70–2 nuclear warheads rated from 1 up to 100 kilotons. Over 2,000 missiles were procured, of which 905 are nuclear-tipped. In addition to these, 380 of the W70–3 enhanced radiation sub-kiloton warhead have been produced. Because of political opposition these have not yet been deployed in Western Europe and are held at the US Army munitions depot at Seneca, New York, the depot specifically designated to support European operations. All of the 692 Lance missiles

deployed in Western Europe are nuclear-tipped. Allocation is divided between 324 for US Army use and the remaining 368 for use by NATO allies. In November 1986 2 Lance launchers and perhaps 12 missiles were deployed to US forces in South Korea, possibly with nuclear warheads.

Lance Follow-on

An improved nuclear-tipped battlefield missile to replace the Lance is regarded as a major priority by NATO military commanders. The prime candidate is a nuclear-tipped version of the Army Tactical Missile System (ATACMS) currently being developed by LTV using an advanced solid-fuel rocket-motor developed by Atlantic Research. ATACMS is 17 feet long and 2 feet in diameter and can be fired from a Multiple Launch Rocket System (MLRS) launcher, carrying a 1,000 lb anti-armour sub-munitions load over a range of up to 130 miles. It uses a Honeywell inertial-guidance package to give accuracies considerably better than Lance. A contract for 50 missiles was awarded in March 1986 and production will commence in 1990 with deployment soon afterwards. In March 1987 it was reported that DoD officials were seeking support from Congress for a nuclear-tipped version of ATACMS. A 400 lb nuclear warhead fitted to ATACMS could give a range in excess of 250 miles and it is reported that 1,000 such missiles are sought by the US Army.

Artillery-fired Atomic Projectiles (AFAPs)

The United States has several thousand nuclear-capable artillery pieces of 2 main bores — 155 mm (6 inch) and 203 mm (8 inch). Many NATO armies use similar guns and have access to AFAPs under US control. The M109 is the main 155 mm piece and the M110 is the main 203 mm piece.

M109 155 mm Howitzer. This 24-ton self-propelled howitzer entered service in 1959 and over 2,000 of several variants have been produced. It can fire the W48 AFAP, first produced in 1963 and rated at 0.1 kilotons, over a range of 11 miles at an initial firing rate of 1 per 15 seconds. Some 3,300 W48 AFAPs have been produced but most have now been withdrawn, with 925 remaining in service. A new warhead, the W82 is now scheduled to enter service in 1990. It will have a yield of up to 2 kilotons and a range of 15 miles and may

be enhanced radiation-capable through the insertion of a module into the AFAP.

M110 203 mm Howitzer. This large self-propelled howitzer has a weight of 28 tons and entered service in 1961 although it has been substantially improved since. Over 1,000 are in service and they can fire the W33 warhead, yielding up to 12 kilotons over a range of 19 miles at a firing rate of 1 every 2 minutes. Of 1,800 rounds originally produced, some 900 remain in service, mainly in Western Europe. The M110 can also fire the new W79 warhead. An initial version of this was neutron-capable but it is now being produced in an orthodox configuration, although it has been reported that the addition of a module can convert it to an ER form. Stocks of the original ER form were not deployed in Western Europe, but were stored at Seneca. Some 300 were produced but some reports suggest that these are being progressively modified to the orthodox form. Some 340 of the different versions of the W79 have been produced and deployment to Western Europe commenced late in 1986.

Atomic Demolition Munitions

Two forms of nuclear mine were produced in the 1960s, a 400 lb mine with three yield options from 1 to 15 kilotons, and a portable 150 lb mine with a 0.01 to 1 kiloton yield. The latter, the Small Atomic Demolition Munition (SADM) remains in service, although no longer permanently stored in Europe. It is deployed with US Special Operations Forces and could be used anywhere in the world including Europe. The SADM was first produced in 1961 and 300 remain in service.

Air Force and Navy Tactical Nuclear Weapons

A variety of anti-ship, anti-submarine and anti-aircraft nuclear-tipped missiles is in service. Both the air force and navy also employ nuclear-capable aircraft and these will be described later.

Genie AIR–2A

The Genie, the world's only air-to-air nuclear-tipped missile, was originally developed in the 1950s for use against massed formations

of bombers and is now being withdrawn from service. It has a 1.5-kiloton W25 warhead and is an unguided missile with a 6 mile range.

Terrier RIM–20

The Terrier is a short-range surface-to-air and surface-to-surface missile originally produced in the early 1950s and still deployed on a number of cruisers, carriers and destroyers. It uses a 2-stage solid-fuel motor and has a range of 21 miles at a speed of Mach 2.5. The Terrier uses a beam-riding guidance system coupled with semi-active homing and carries a W45 warhead rated at under a kiloton. There are 285 still in service.

Standard 2 RIM–67B

This Terrier replacement is already widely in service with a conventional warhead. After protracted financial problems, the planned nuclear-tipped form is now likely to enter US Navy service by 1989. The Standard 2 is half the size of the Terrier but has a much greater range — around 65 miles — and will carry the W81 low-kiloton-range warhead. Perhaps 350 of a total procurement of 2,000 will be nuclear-armed and the missile will be substantially more accurate than the Terrier. It is seen primarily as a defence against nuclear-armed anti-ship cruise missiles.

ASROC RUR–5A

This was developed by Honeywell in the late 1950s, entering service in 1961. It is an unguided but range-controlled single-stage missile some 15 feet in length and capable of delivering conventional torpedoes or nuclear depth-charges over a distance of up to 7 miles. The nuclear-armed version carries the sub-kiloton-yield W44 warhead and is intended for ASW use. There are still 575 of this version in service on a wide range of frigates, cruisers and destroyers. ASROC is being upgraded into a new version for deployment in a vertical launch system but it is not yet clear whether this deployment mode will involve the nuclear-armed version.

SUBROC UUM-44A

This Goodyear Aerospace missile is fired from a submarine's torpedo tube in encapsulated form, propels itself to the surface, travels in a ballistic trajectory through the air for up to 35 miles and then delivers a W55 nuclear warhead rated at 1 to 5 kilotons. Around 285 are in service on SSN and these will be retired by 1989 or 1990 pending the introduction of the Sea Lance.

Sea Lance

This Boeing/Gould replacement for SUBROC will also be produced in a version able to be fired by Mark 41 launchers on a number of classes of cruisers and destroyers. It will thus partially replace ASROC as well as SUBROC. The nuclear version of Sea Lance will probably have a low kiloton yield but the main difference will lie in the range — perhaps as great as 100 miles, some 3 times that of SUBROC. Full-scale engineering development commenced late in 1986 and 50 missiles were ordered for flight-testing.

Nuclear-capable Strike Aircraft and Associated Munitions

The US Air Force and Navy deploy a wide range of nuclear-capable strike aircraft, in addition to the intermediate-range aircraft such as the F–111 and F–15E already described. All of the following aircraft are in service in conventional and nuclear roles and it is rarely possible to indicate which numbers are assigned to the latter role. Table 3 (below) lists the total numbers together with unrefuelled combat radius and whether the planes can be refuelled in the air.

Table 4 (below) indicates the range of bombs which can be deployed with each aircraft or helicopter and also shows the maximum number of each bomb which can be carried on a sortie. The table excludes strategic and intermediate aircraft and the heavy B53 bomb. A brief description of the bombs follows:

— *B28.* This is still a widely deployed strategic and tactical thermonuclear bomb originally developed in the 1950s and first produced in 1958. The B28 comes in 5 different yields from 70 kilotons to 1.45 megatons but any one bomb has only

Table 3 Number and specifications of US nuclear-capable strike aircraft

Aircraft	Numbers	Combat radius (miles)	Aerial refuelling
A–4 Skyhawk	396	400	Yes
A–6 Intruder	187	870	Yes
A–7 Corsair	633	800	Yes
AV–8B Harrier	41	700	Yes
F–4 Phantom	882	600	Yes
F–15 Eagle	685	1,060	Yes
F–16 Fighting Falcon	912	575	Yes
F/A–18 Hornet	234	415	Yes
P–3 Orion	362	1,550	No
S–3 Viking	110	1,100	Yes
SH–3 Sea King	102	300	No

Table 4 Quantity and range of bombs which can be deployed by US nuclear-capable strike aircraft

	Bomb				
Aircraft	B28	B43	B57	B61	B83
A–4 Skyhawk	1	1	1	1	?1
A–6 Intruder	3	3	3	3	?3
A–7 Corsair	4	4	4	4	?4
AV–8B Harrier	—	—	1	1	—
F–4 Phantom	1	3	3	3	?1
F–15 Eagle	—	?2	—	?2	—
F–16 Fighting Falcon	—	2	—	2	?2
F/A–18 Hornet	—	—	2	2	—
P–3 Orion	—	—	3	—	—
S–3 Viking	—	—	4	—	—
SH–3 Sea King	—	—	?4	—	—

one yield. The bomb itself weighs 2,000 to 2,500 lb depending on configuration. Around 1,000 remain in service.

— *B43.* This bomb was first produced in 1961 and is now being replaced by the B61 and B83 bombs. Over 1,000 having been withdrawn in the past three years, 925 now remain in service. The B43 can be carried by most nuclear-capable aircraft, weighs just over 2,000 lb and has a yield of 1 megaton.

— *B57.* Around 1,200 of this bomb are deployed in air-, surface-

and sub-surface-burst variants, the last-named as an ASW system. It is a small bomb, weighing under 700 lb and yielding from less than 1 to 20 kilotons. It is being replaced by the B61 bomb.

— *B61.* Several versions of this bomb have been produced, with the most recent still being in production. The B61–0, –1 and –7 versions are essentially strategic and have a yield of 1 to 500 kilotons, with 1,000 deployed. The B61–2, –3, –4 and –5 versions yield up to 345 kilotons and are used in the tactical role — 2,150 of these are in service. The B61 weighs 800 lb and later versions can be dropped at high speed from heights of 50 feet with an accuracy reported to be as low as 300 feet CEP. Yield can be selected by the pilot after take-off.

— *B83.* This is the main new strategic bomb and was first produced in 1983. Out of a likely production run of 2,500 1,000 have already been produced, and it will be deployed on some tactical aircraft such as the A–7 and F–16 as well as strategic aircraft. The B83 weighs 2,400 lb and has a yield of up to 1.2 megatons. Parachute-assisted delivery allows accurate single-pass high-speed attacks at altitudes as low as 150 feet.

In addition to these bombs, the US Air Force is seeking a new short-range stand-off missile for tactical use, this being additional to the SRAM 2 which is to serve as a defence suppression strategic weapon. The weapon is termed the *Modular Air-to-surface Missile* (MASM) but range, speed and warhead-yield are not yet known. If it enters full-scale development, IOC is likely to be in the early 1990s.

Carrier-based Aircraft

Six of the nuclear-capable aircraft listed (A–4, A–6, A–7, AV–8B, F/A–18 and SH–3) can operate from aircraft-carriers of which the United States has 15, all exceeding 60,000 tons displacement. Thirteen normally have air wings embarked, one carrier being for training and one undergoing long-term refit. The US carriers give an unrivalled long distance tactical air force projection capability and this includes tactical nuclear bombs and nuclear depth-bombs. A carrier air wing will include perhaps 34 attack and ASW aircraft and 6 ASW helicopters, all nuclear-capable. All fixed-wing nuclear-

capable aircraft operating from carriers can be refuelled in the air, and each carrier has 4 tanker aircraft for this purpose. The United States plans to operate 15 carrier air wings by the early 1990s.

Future Tactical Aircraft

The US Air Force has 2 new combat aircraft under development and the US Navy has one. While neither of the USAF planes is likely to be deployed initially in a nuclear-capable role, previous experience suggests that this will follow.

The US Air Force's 'stealth' fighter, built by Lockheed, has been flying for several years and reliable sources indicate that perhaps 45 are now in service. It is unofficially designated the *F–19*. The *Advanced Tactical Fighter* (ATF) is at a much earlier stage of development and will not enter service until 1995. Around 750 of this Mach 2 plane will be deployed.

The US Navy plans to have prototypes of its *Advanced Combat Aircraft* (ACA) ready for competitive fly-offs by 1990, with a mid-1990s IOC. The ACA will be intended primarily to replace the A–6 Intruder, and about 450 will be built.

Soviet Union

The Soviet Union continues to develop and deploy a wide range of strategic, intermediate and tactical nuclear weapons. All 3 legs of the strategic triad are being developed, including 2 ICBMs, 2 SLBMs and a strategic penetrating bomber. While force levels of the SS–20 intermediate-range ballistics missile have been frozen, a follow-on missile is being flight-tested. A range of cruise missiles is under development, there appears to be increasing attention being paid to tactical nuclear weapons such as AFAPs, and a number of new strike aircraft are likely eventually to be deployed in a nuclear-capable configuration.

There is some evidence of a slowing down of deployment rates of some weapons systems such as the SS–25 ICBM, the Bear H stand-off strategic bomber and possibly the *Delta IV* fleet ballistic missile submarine, but this may be due to exaggerated expectations by US intelligence sources in the early 1980s. Two more definite indications of a possible change of direction are the freezing of SS–20 deployments and the self-imposed nuclear test ban from August 1985 to March 1987.

Even so, these aspects should be seen in the context of a general build-up of strategic forces which continues to give a substantial net increase in deliverable warheads each year.

Intercontinental Ballistic Missiles

The ICBM leg of the Soviet strategic triad continues to be the most important, with well over half the strategic warheads carried by ICBMs. While the MIRVing of the SLBM force and the eventual deployment of the Blackjack bomber may slightly diminish the relative importance of the ICBM force it will remain the dominant component for at least a decade.

SS–11 (Sego)

This is the oldest ICBM in the Soviet inventory, having first been deployed in 1966. For most of the past twenty years it has been the mainstay of the Soviet ICBM force in terms of numbers of missiles (but not warheads) but is now being withdrawn as new missiles are deployed. It is a 3-stage liquid-fuel missile, 64 feet long and with a range of 5,500 to 6,500 miles depending on warhead configuration.

The SS–11 might correctly be described as a Variable-Range Ballistic Missile (VRBM) because, prior to SS–20 IRBM deployments, a part of the SS–11 force was reported to be targeted on Western Europe. The SS–11 has a limited silo reload capacity, probably taking several days.

The SS–11 Mod 1 version carried a 950-kiloton warhead and had a CEP of 4,600 feet. Withdrawal of this version is now complete. Mod 2 carries a single-megaton warhead and Mod 3 an MRV system with 3 100- to 300-kiloton warheads. As the SS–24 and SS–25 ICBMs come into service the 400 Mod 2 and 3 versions of the SS–11 still operational are being withdrawn on a one-for-one basis. At its peak there were 960 SS–11s deployed in the early 1970s.

SS–13 (Savage)

This appears to have been the first attempt by the Soviet Union to develop a solid-fuel ICBM, deployment commencing in 1966. It was developed by the Nadiradze design bureau and was probably aimed at being as effective as the early US Minuteman series in terms of reaction time. It is silo-launched and has a length of 65 feet and a range of 6,200 miles carrying a single 600-kiloton warhead. CEP is 6,000 feet.

The SS–13 did not fulfil expectations and only 60 were deployed, these remaining in service in the Yoshkar Ola missile field although they are likely to be replaced by the SS–25. The Soviet Union persistently claims that the SS–25 is a modification of the SS–13, allowable under the SALT II agreement.

SS–16

This ICBM was developed in the early 1970s, also by the Nadiradze bureau, possibly as a replacement for the inferior SS–13. It was

planned as a limited-range (5,500 miles) ICBM using solid fuel and carrying a MIRV front-end, although it was only tested with a single re-entry vehicle. It was intended for silo or mobile launch in the Eastern Soviet Union but experienced considerable development problems, possibly with the first of its 3 stages. The upper 2 stages were developed into the SS–20 IRBM and successfully deployed from 1977 onwards.

Development problems may have motivated the Soviet Union to agree to its exclusion from deployment under SALT II rules, but up to 60 may have been produced and put into store. Persistent reports from defence sources in the United States in the early 1980s claimed that 100 to 200 SS–16s had been deployed at Plesetsk in violation of SALT II, but in March 1986 the US Arms Control and Disarmament Agency reported that they had been removed in 1985. Independent analysts mostly doubt that they were ever deployed.

SS–17 (Spanker)

The SS–17 was the first of a group of 3 ICBMs deployed by the Soviet Union in the 1970s, 150 of this missile replacing SS–11s in silos. It was developed by the Yangel design bureau and first deployed in 1975, over a similar time-scale to the SS–19. It is not regarded as a successful missile and the deployment of as many as 150 may be due to its being cold-launched whereas the SS–19 is hot-launched. Bureaucratic rivalry with the Cholomei design bureau, developers of the SS–19, may also be relevant.

The SS–17 is 80 feet in length, has a range of 6,200 miles and has storable liquid motors. It has been deployed in three forms. Mod 1 had 4 750-kiloton warheads and a CEP of, at best, 1,500 feet, and Mod 2 was a single warhead missile rated at 6 megatons. Both have now been replaced by the 4-MIRV Mod 3, first deployed in 1982, fitted with 500-kiloton warheads and having a CEP of, at best, 1,200 feet. It is assumed that all 150 SS–17s are deployed with the Mod 3 system.

SS–18 (Satan)

The SS–18 remains, by a large margin, the world's largest ballistic missile and replaced the early SS–9 Scarp missile on a one-for-one basis in the late 1970s, 308 being deployed in silos, some of which are reported to be hardened to 6,000 p.s.i. The SS–18 is a 2-stage

missile using storable liquid motors and having a length of 120 feet and a maximum range of 6,500 miles depending on payload. It has been deployed in at least four forms, with a possible fifth version under development. Analysts assume that all 308 missiles carry the Mod 4 system. Specifications of the four versions of the SS–18 are as follows:

— *Mod 1*, deployed in the mid-1970s, was a single-warhead system with a 20- to 27-megaton warhead and a CEP of around 1,450 feet.
— *Mod 2* became operational in 1976 with 8 900-kiloton warheads in a MIRV system with a similar CEP to the single-warhead Mod 1 but a more limited range.
— *Mod 3* appears to have been an enhanced version of Mod 1 with a longer range and an accuracy of 1,150 feet CEP. This would have considerable potential against hardened command and control centres, but it is assumed that all have been withdrawn in favour of Mod 4 warheads
— *Mod 4* is broadly similar to Mod 2 but carries 10 500-kiloton warheads and has a CEP of around 850 feet (although other sources are more vague at 'under 1,000 feet'). US sources claim that the SS–18 Mod 4 has the throw-weight potential for up to 24 warheads.

While the consensus view is that all 308 SS–18s have the Mod 4 warheads, it may be that a small number of single-warhead Mod 3s remain in service for attacks on deep underground command and control centres.

US DoD sources consider that double targeting of US ICBM's silos by SS–18 warheads would destroy 65 to 80 per cent of silos while leaving 1,000 warheads unused. This assumes that the accuracy figures, based on US intelligence estimates, are correct and not exaggerated.

SS–19 (Stiletto)

This missile is similar in size, range and propulsion to the SS–17 but is hot-launched from its silo. It appears to have been considered more successful than the SS–17, with 360 deployed from 1974 onwards. It is a 2-stage missile, 74 feet long and with a maximum range of 6,000 miles. There have been three versions:

- *Mod 1* was first deployed in 1974 carrying a 6-MIRV system of 550-kiloton warheads and a CEP reported to be 1,250 feet. All have been replaced by the Mod 3.
- *Mod 2* was first deployed in 1979 and carried a single warhead variously estimated at between 5 and 10 megatons, having a CEP of around 1,000 feet. Unconfirmed reports suggest that this, too, has been replaced by the Mod 3.
- *Mod 3* was first deployed in 1982, also with a 6-MIRV system of 550-kiloton warheads and a reported CEP of 1,000 feet. In 1984 US sources revised the CEP down to 1,200 feet. This, in turn, casts doubt on the published accuracy figures for the earlier versions of the SS–19.

The downward revision of the Mod 3 CEP suggests that its potential against hard targets is limited. It is probable that up to 60 SS–19s are targeted on Western Europe and South East Asia, thus following a practice employed with the SS–11.

SS–24 (Scalpel)

In October 1982, the Soviet Union commenced testing a new ICBM, originally designated PL–04 but now known as the SS–24. It is a 3-stage solid-fuel missile similar in size to the US M–X Peacekeeper. Of the first 10 test-flights, 7 ended in failure and the missile has had a protracted and difficult development. Initial deployment was expected in 1986 but was delayed. In early 1987 it was reported that 10 missiles had finally been deployed, possibly at 2 sites in the European Soviet Union. The SS–24 carries 8 to 10 100-kiloton warheads and has an accuracy of 600 feet CEP, although this is probably from a silo. The missile is intended for deployment in silos and on mobile launchers which can operate on ordinary railways. Initial deployment is on mobile launchers with silo deployment before the end of the decade.

Production of the SS–24 appears to be slow, probably a consequence of persistent development problems. With a CEP of 600 feet and carrying 100-kiloton warheads it is markedly inferior to the US M–X Peacekeeper and probably even inferior to the SS–18 Mod 4. It is reported that a new version of the missile is already under development and this may be part of a major effort to overcome earlier problems.

SS–25 (Sickle)

This is a light missile, similar in size to the US Minuteman III but deployed exclusively on a wheeled launch vehicle broadly similar to that of the SS–20 IRBM. The SS–25 was originally designated PL–05 and deployment appears to have commenced in 1985 or early 1986. In the period up to March 1986 70 were deployed, but in the following 12 months only 30 followed.

The SS–25 is a 3-stage solid-fuel missile 59 feet long and capable of carrying a single 550-kiloton warhead over a range of 6,500 miles. Its large transporter-erector-launch vehicles are housed in groups of large unhardened garages with sliding roofs, apprently to permit rapid firing, although dispersal must be the key to survivability. The Soviet Union claims that the SS–25 is merely a variant of the SS–13 and therefore allowable under SALT II conditions. The United States persistently denies this. SS–11 missiles are being dismantled to compensate for SS–25 deployments which have been concentrated initially around Plesetsk, the site of the SS–13 deployments.

It is reported that a new version of the SS–25 is already under development and will be deployed with a 3-MIRV warhead. These will, presumably, be rated lower than the 550-kiloton single warhead, and might use the SS–24 warhead. Accuracy when launched from the pre-surveyed sites is similar to that of the SS–24 at 600 feet CEP.

SS–X–26

A large new missile, possibly an SS–18 replacement, commenced flight-testing in April 1986, although the first flight ended abruptly when the first-stage solid-fuelled booster exploded on ignition, partially destroying the launch-site. A second test later in the year also failed, but the third attempt, in December 1986, was a success. US sources have used a preliminary designation of TT–09, but the SS–X–26 designation is expected to be confirmed. The missile may be deployed in strength within five to six years, replacing the SS–18. It is likely to carry a 10-MIRV system but may have a throw-weight potential for a much larger number of RVs. The Soviet Union is likely to insist that it is simply a Mod 5 SS–18, but if it is a solid-fuel system this would suggest otherwise.

SS–X–27

There are persistent reports of a further ICBM being developed but these could refer to modified versions of the SS–24 or SS–25. One unconfirmed source suggests a Minuteman III-type light ICBM but it is by no means clear that this would be an entirely new system. Early reports of yet another heavy ICBM being developed may result from a confusion with the SS–X–26.

Submarine-launched Ballistic Missiles

The Soviet Union lagged many years behind the United States in producing large SSBN and SLBMs, and was also slow in introducing MIRVed SLBMs. This inferiority was partially compensated by building over 60 SSBN, substantially more than the US, although all but the latest of these are regarded as far less reliable than their US counterparts. US SSBN commonly spend over 60 per cent of their time at sea, whereas their Soviet counterparts spend less than 20 per cent of their time at sea. In recent years the Soviet Union has produced large long-range SLBMs capable of being launched from close to home waters in 'sanctuaries' such as the Barents Sea and the Sea of Okhotsk. It is now engaged in producing a number of MIRVed SLBMs and their introduction will substantially increase the number of warheads in the strategic inventory.

SS–N–6 (Serb)

The Serb was the mainstay of the Soviet SLBM force for many years, but more recent MIRVed missiles now carry far more warheads. It is analogous to Polaris although with a shorter range and liquid-fuelled motors. The 2,000-mile-range missile has 2 stages, a CEP of, at best, 3,000 feet and 2 warheads variously reported to yield 200 or 500 kilotons. The relatively short range of the SS–N–6 means that the submarine has to patrol close to the US coast where it is vulnerable to US anti-submarine defences.

The SS–N–6 is carried on *Yankee I*-class SSBN, and the 18 currently in service carry 288 missiles. One *Yankee* boat was lost in the North Atlantic on 6 October 1986 after a fire and explosion in one of its missile tubes. The 16 missiles with their 32 thermonuclear warheads have not been recovered.

SS–N–8 (Sawfly)

This is a large missile, 42 feet in length and capable of delivering a single 800-kiloton warhead over a 5,000 mile range, enabling it to launch from close to home waters. It is carried in *Delta I* and *Delta II* SSBN. There are 18 of the former in service, each with 12 launch tubes, and 4 of the latter with 16 tubes. Together with 2 diesel-powered missile submarines, an *Hotel III*-class trials boat with 6 missiles and a *Golf III* class with a similar number, there are 292 SS–N–8 missiles available for deployment. The considerable length of the missile requires a bulge in the *Delta* boats extending aft of the conning tower.

SS–NX–17 (Snipe)

The SS–NX–17 was first test-fired in 1975 and has undergone sporadic trials on a single modified *Yankee II* submarine with 12 launch tubes ever since. It was probably intended as a replacement for the SS–N–8 which, while effective in range, suffered the draw-back of liquid-fuel motors of dubious reliability. The SS–NX–17 is still experimental, as the designation implies. It uses a solid-fuel system and has a post-boost vehicle implying some kind of MIRV system, although it has only been reported with a single 500-kiloton warhead. Its range of 2,400 miles and accuracy of 5,000 feet CEP suggest a failed attempt to produce a solid-fuel SLBM.

SS–N–18 (Stingray)

This missile was first deployed in 1978 and may be regarded as little more than a modification of the SS–N–8, with more reliable liquid-fuel motors and a post-boost vehicle giving MIRV potential. Early missiles were fitted with a single 450-kiloton warhead and had a range of 5,000 miles or carried a 3-MIRV system with 200-kiloton warheads and a 4,000 mile range. The Mod 3 version, now widely in service, carries a 7-MIRV system, again with 200-kiloton warheads and a 4,000 mile range. The CEP of the 3-MIRV version was a very poor 5,000 feet, but that of the 7-MIRV system has been reported at just under 3,000 feet. This improvement is still well outside that of the US Poseidon SLBM, a 10- to 14-MIRV missile with a 1,500 feet CEP (but 40-kiloton warheads) first deployed eight years before the SS–N–18 Mod 3.

SS–N–20 (Sturgeon)

In developing the SS–N–20, the Soviet Union finally succeeded in producing a solid-fuel SLBM. It is carried in the *Typhoon*-class SSBN, the world's largest submarine. The SS–N–20 is the world's largest SLBM and has a throw-weight large enough to enable it to carry 6 to 9 100-kiloton warheads in a MIRV system over a 5,100 mile range. The *Typhoon* boat has a displacement of around 25,000 tons and carries 20 missiles in launch tubes located, unusually, forward of the sail. Early assessments credited the *Typhoon* with a maximum speed of 30 knots, but this has been downgraded by some analysts to, at most, 24 knots. In any case, the function of the class is to patrol close to home waters, often under the Arctic ice. By mid-1987 there were 4 *Typhoon* boats in service, all based at Gremikha, some 200 miles east of Murmansk. A further boat was launched late in 1986 entering service during 1987. There are probably 2 or 3 more boats being built and a class of perhaps 10 is likely by the mid-1990s. This is half the number of the slightly smaller *Ohio*-class boats in the United States, but the Soviet Union is also constructing the *Delta IV* class at the same time.

Although the SS–N–20 is an entirely new missile, it does not appear to be particularly accurate. While a marked improvement on previous SLBMs, the SS–N–20 is reported to have a CEP of around 1,600 feet which is markedly inferior to the US Trident D5 missile due in service in 1989, and even inferior to older US SLBMs such as the Poseidon C3 and Trident C4.

SS–N–23 (Skiff)

This is essentially a new version of the SS–N–18, probably with an increased throw-weight but without any increase in accuracy. It was originally reported to carry a 7-MIRV system but more recent reports suggest a 10-MIRV system probably with relatively low-yield warheads. It is deployed in the new *Delta IV*-class SSBN, a variant of the well-established *Delta III*. *Delta*-class boats were expected to cease production in the 1980s, but the introduction of the *Delta IV* indicates long-term plans for further deployments. Four have been launched, each carrying 16 missiles. By early 1987 2 were in service. They will probably be built at the rate of 1 a year, and may have been ordered, together with the SS–N–23, as a hedge against the failure of the solid-fuel SS–N–20. With the success of

the missile apparently assured, the *Delta IV* class may be limited to around 8 boats, especially if a new SSBN is under development as some reports indicate.

Future SLBM Developments

According to US intelligence sources, a new class of submarine is due to enter service in the early 1990s. As the *Typhoon* boat is an entirely new design, and also a very expensive boat, it is probable that a new SSBN would be a 16-tube design. Sources also believe that a new version of the SS–N–20 is under development for flight-testing before the end of the decade. An SS–N–23 follow-on is also possible in the early 1990s but as that missile is already a modification of the SS–N–18 it is likely that a quite new type of missile might be developed, certainly with solid-fuel motors. It is unlikely that the Soviet Union will be able to develop SLBMs with an accuracy sufficient to give a hard-target capability before the mid-1990s.

Long-range Bombers and Associated Missiles

The Soviet Union has always been less reliant on strategic bombers than the United States, the only significant long-range bombers to have been deployed since 1950 being the Bear and Bison, capable of delivering gravity bombs and a range of stand-off missiles described below. These bombers have a much lower load-carrying capacity than, for example, the B–52 or B–1B and, as the stand-off missiles are larger and heavier, the capabilities do not compare favourably with the US equivalent.

An attempt *was* made, in the 1960s, to produce a very large heavy bomber, the Myasischev M–50, but this was only produced in prototype and never deployed operationally. There has been much heavier investment in medium-range bombers, which are described separately. One, the Backfire, is theoretically capable of reaching the United States with aerial refuelling, although the limited number of tanker aircraft in the Soviet strategic inventory precludes this as a significant strategic weapon.

During the 1980s, two new developments suggest that the Soviet Union is at last placing a greater emphasis on strategic bombers. One is the development of the AS–15 air-launched cruise missile

linked to a launch aircraft, a new variant of the Bear bomber. The other is the flight-testing of a large supersonic penetration bomber, the Blackjack. While neither the AS–15 nor the Blackjack compare very favourably with their US equivalents, they do represent a significant new component to the Soviet strategic arsenal.

Tupolev Tu–95 (Bear)

The Bear was first flown in public in 1955 and was initially deployed carrying free-fall thermonuclear bombs. A number of types have been produced for penetration, stand-off and even ECM and ASW roles. The Bear is a very large swept-wing plane powered by 4 turboprop engines giving it a speed of 500 m.p.h. and a range of just under 8,000 miles with an 11-ton bomb load, or rather shorter with a maximum 18-ton load. Early versions carried the AS–3 Kangaroo missile but 40 have been modified to carry the more recent AS–4 Kitchen, these now being termed Bear G planes. Up to 1984, around 100 Bear bombers were deployed in the strategic role, carrying 1 or 2 free-fall bombs or up to 3 missiles.

In 1984, the Bear H was first deployed, capable of carrying the new AS–15 cruise missile. Each plane carries 2 missiles on each of 2 inboard wing pylons. Two more may be carried in the bomb bay but this has not been confirmed. In 1984–5 25 planes were deployed, 15 the following year and perhaps 12 in 1986–7. This indicates a slowing down, probably to an annual production rate of 10. The Bear H may well be a temporary solution to the problem of providing launch aircraft for long-range stand-off missiles pending the eventual deployment of the delayed Blackjack bomber.

During 1986, Bear H planes were frequently reported on the fringes of Canadian and even US air space and it became apparent that the deployment of Soviet strategic bombers with long-range stand-off missiles might require a general upgrading of US and Canadian air defences. By mid-1987 there were probably 65 Bear H aircraft in service with 260 to 390 AS–15 cruise missiles. While substantial, this compares with 1,700 US ALCM missiles on 140 B–52s.

Myasischev M–4 (Bison)

The Bison is of a similar vintage to the B–52, and is a large subsonic 4-jet long-range bomber which entered service in 1956 and carries

free-fall thermonuclear weapons rather than stand-off missiles. It has not been regarded as a successful bomber owing to range and load limitations, and only 20 remain in service in the strategic role although others serve as tankers and ECM aircraft. It is likely to be withdrawn from service by 1990.

Tu–X

A derivative of the TU–144 passenger jet has been reported as under development as a supersonic long-range cruise missile carrier. Reports persist but the development of the Bear H and flight-testing of the Blackjack make this additional project unlikely.

Tu–? (Blackjack)

The Blackjack is a large, supersonic variable-geometry long-range penetration bomber which may also be deployed with air-launched cruise missiles. It is believed to come from the Tupolev design bureau and was originally thought to be a scaled-up Backfire. It is now recognised as an entirely new design, substantially larger and probably faster than the US B–1B but with a similar range.

The Blackjack has a length of about 155 feet and is probably powered by 4 turbofans giving it a maximum speed of Mach 2.0 and an unrefuelled range of 8,600 miles. Its maximum weapons load has been reported at 16 tons compared with over 28 tons for the B–1B. The size and configuration of the weapons bay and the number of load points has not been reported and this will help to determine the number of ALCMs which could be carried. This could number 6 to 12 in the case of the AS–15.

Flight-testing is believed to have commenced in 1982 and initial deployment was expected by 1985. By early 1987, 5 Blackjacks were involved in flight-testing although 1 crashed in May. The IOC was estimated at 1988. There do, therefore, appear to have been delays in producing the Blackjack. It is assumed that full-scale production will have begun by 1988, and that at least 120 planes will be built to replace early Bear and Bison bombers, with the Bear H ALCM carrier remaining in service into the 1990s.

If large-scale production of perhaps 30 planes a year was undertaken, the combination of large numbers of Blackjacks with bombs and AS–15 missiles would, together with the Bear H force, result in a substantial bomber leg to the Soviet strategic triad.

AS–3 (Kangaroo)

The Kangaroo is a very high-altitude cruise missile with a range of about 400 miles and a speed of Mach 2.0. It was first deployed in 1961 and has a length of 48 feet and a wingspan of 30 feet. It is thus larger than some fighters and each Bear bomber can carry just 1 missile. It carries a megaton-range warhead although it is theoretically dual-capable. Different sources suggest that 70 to 100 Kangaroos remain in service but recent reports suggest that it is rapidly being withdrawn from service with the Bear in favour of the AS–4. One source lists the Kangaroo as subsonic.

AS–4 (Kitchen)

While the Kitchen was first produced in 1962 it is regarded as a more sophisticated missile than the Kangaroo. It is powered by a liquid-fuel rocket-motor and has a length of 37 feet and a wingspan of 10 feet. The Kitchen has a high-altitude range of around 200 miles at Mach 3.5 and has been used primarily in the anti-shipping role, carried by Blinder and Backfire bombers but, more recently, by Bears as well. Different sources credit it with either a 200-kiloton or 1-megaton warhead. As many as 650 AS–4s have been deployed, but many have now been withdrawn and numbers probably total around 450.

AS–6 (Kingfish)

The Kingfish entered service in 1977 and has a length of 33 feet, a wingspan of 8 feet and a launch-weight of about 5 tons. It has a high-altitude range of around 200 miles, flying at 60,000 feet before diving onto its target, and is rocket powered, carrying a 350-kiloton thermonuclear warhead or a high-explosive warhead. Around 800 are in service primarily as specialised anti-ship weapons. Some sources suggest that the AS–6 did not fulfill expectations, which is why so many AS–4s are still deployed, but it was more likely developed specifically as an anti-ship missile. It is not clear whether any are deployed in a strategic role. The Kingfish combines inertial mid-course guidance and active terminal homing. It can fly in a low-altitude mode with a reported range of 120 miles.

AS–X–11/AS–X–13

Various reports suggest an attempt to develop a replacement for the AS–4. The designation AS–X–13 is now most commonly used. The missile is reported to have a length of 16.5 feet and a range of 500 miles at Mach 3.5. It is not reported to have been deployed and it is possible that it may be superseded by the AS–15 and BL–10, although the former is subsonic and the latter, while supersonic, is a very large and much longer-range missile.

AS–15 (Kent)

The AS–15 is the Soviet equivalent of the ALCM and came into service on Bear H bombers two years later than the ALCM, in 1984. The Kent is similar in form to the much smaller ALCM and carries a 250-kiloton warhead. It has a length of 23 feet, a wingspan of 10 feet 8 inches, and is normally carried 4 per plane on the Bear, although 2 more might be carried internally. The Kent is presumed to be powered by a small jet engine and has a speed of Mach 0.6, rather slower than its US equivalent. Most sources credit it with an 1,850 mile range, but one authoritative estimate puts it at 1,000 miles. It is credited with having a TERCOM-style guidance system giving a CEP of 150 feet but this has not been confirmed. Production may now be around 100 per year with the stockpile being built up pending the deployment of the Blackjack.

BL–10

There have been a number of reports of a large supersonic stand-off missile under development as a replacement for the AS–4, with a range of 2,000 miles being indicated. Little further information has come out and it is probably that the BL–10 is an experimental system which could be developed as an AS–15 alternative should that experience problems in deployment.

Ballistic Missile Defences

The Soviet Union has a wide range of programmes cocerned with defences against ballistic missiles, most of which may not be nuclear-armed and would therefore be beyond the scope of this

report. An early form of ballistic missile defence, based on the Galosh nuclear-armed missile, was deployed around Moscow from 1964 onwards and consisted of 64 launchers in 4 above-ground complexes.

The whole system is currently being upgraded following the withdrawal of half of the Galosh launchers in the early 1980s. The new system will have the 100 launchers allowed under the ABM treaty and will consist of a 2-layered system of exoatmospheric and endoatmospheric interceptor missiles, not unlike the Spartan/Sprint system deployed briefly and unsuccessfully by the United States in the 1970s. Both layers of the system are likely to be nuclear-armed and it is not clear how the effects of nuclear detonations on communications systems will be avoided.

ABM–1B (Galosh)

Thirty-two of these missiles remain deployed in 2 complexes. Each missile has a range of 200 miles and carries a substantial 3-megaton warhead. Its position allows for the protection of Moscow and ICBM fields in the vicinity, but Western observers regard the protection offered as rudimentary at best.

ABM–2

Originally designated SH–04, this is believed to be a modified and improved version of the ABM–1B. It is still likely to be fitted with a substantial thermonuclear warhead, and its main features are an improved guidance system and the ability of the missile motor to be stopped and started several times, thus providing a 'loitering' capability enabling command facilities to identify decoys.

ABM–3

Originally designated SH–08, this is a much shorter-range rapid acceleration hypersonic missile designed to destroy incoming warheads which have penetrated the ABM–2 defences. It is likely to be nuclear-armed.

The ABM–2/ABM–3 combination is expected to total 100 launchers, with US sources claiming a silo-based system involving reload capabilities. Some sources suggested completion of the new system by 1987, but a completion date towards the end of the decade

is now considered more likely.

Nuclear-Powered ABM Devices

The United States is committed to research into directional nuclear warheads including the X-ray laser and hypervelocity pellet generators. US DoD assessments of the relative sophistication of US and Soviet nuclear warhead design credit the Soviet Union as being equal to the United States. Independent analysts tend to doubt this, and there is evidence that in matters such as warhead miniaturisation, the United States has a substantial lead.

Even so, it would be surprising if the Soviet Union were not also engaged in programmes to develop directional warheads. When the Soviet Union resumed nuclear testing early in 1987 after its self-imposed 19-month moratorium, the third test was reported to be concerned with an experimental warhead rather than development of an existing programme. The extent and nature of the Soviet test programme in the late 1980s may indicate the extent to which it is expending resources on novel warhead designs.

Intermediate Nuclear Forces

The Soviet Union has had intermediate- and medium-range nuclear forces available for targeting Western Europe and South East Asia since 1959. It has also developed a number of bombers intended for theatre use. The missile force is dominated by the SS–20 and the main bomber is the Tu–26 Backfire.

SS–4 (Sandal)

This relatively short-range missile was initially deployed in 1959 and carries a single thermonuclear warhead variously rated at between 1 and 1.2 megatons. As many as 600 were deployed from the early 1960s onwards, and attempts to base SS–4s in Cuba precipitated the 1962 Cuban Missile Crisis. The SS–4 is 69 feet long, weighs 27 tons on launch and has a range of 1,200 miles. Its liquid-fuel motor is difficult to maintain and takes up to 8 hours to prepare for firing. Some missiles are silo-based but most have used open launch-pads clustered in groups of 4 and highly vulnerable to pre-emption. The SS–4 is highly inaccurate with a CEP of 7,500 feet.

In addition to the SS–4, the Soviet Union deployed the longer-range SS–5 from 1961 to 1984 and this had broadly similar limitations to the SS–4. As a result, considerable effort was spent in developing replacement missiles during the 1960s and early 1970s. The *SS–14 (Scapegoat)* was intended as a mobile solid-fuel replacement for the SS–4, based on the upper 2 stages of the SS–13 ICBM. The SS–14 may have been deployed briefly but was not a successful system and was quickly withdrawn. A succesor to the SS–5, the *SS–15*, was flight-tested but never deployed. Consequently, the SS–4 and SS–5 remained in service far longer than expected, with perhaps 100 SS–4s still deployed in early 1987.

SS–20 (Saber)

With the SS–20, the Soviet Union finally succeeded in producing a solid-fuel intermediate-range missile. It was developed from the top 2 stages of the SS–16 ICBM by the Nadiradze Bureau and took ten years to develop, deployment starting in 1977. The SS–20 is 52 feet long and has a launch-weight of 25 tons. There are three versions but only the first is believed to be deployed. The other two (Mod 1 and Mod 3) are probably experimental. The three versions have the following specifications:

— *Mod 1* carries a single warhead, variously reported as having a yield of 650 kilotons or 1.0 or 1.5 megatons, and has a range of 3,100 miles.
— *Mod 2* has a 3-MIRV system of 150-kiloton warheads and a 3,100 mile range.
— *Mod 3* has a single 50-kiloton lightweight warhead giving the missile a substantially increased range of 4,600 miles, bringing it within range of the continental United States if deployed in Eastern Siberia.

Mod 1 may have been deployed briefly but all the indications are that the 3-MIRV Mod 2 is the standard form of the missile.

When launched from fixed sites under experimental conditions, an accuracy of 1,300 feet CEP may be achieved, but deployment to pre-surveyed field sites results in a CEP of 2,250 feet. Thus the missile is a considerable improvement on the SS–4 and SS–5 but does not have a hard-target capability. It is actually considerably less accurate than US SLBMs such as Poseidon, some 400 warheads

of which are assigned to NATO for theatre nuclear targeting. The SS–20 cannot compare with the terminally-guided Pershing 2.

The SS–20 is described as a 3-MIRV missile but there have been reports that it is effectively a limited MIRV missile in that the MIRV bus was developed initially for ICBM use and warhead separation over the reduced IRBM range results in a very limited footprint for the 3 warheads. This limitation might be a partial explanation for the Soviet Union being prepared to dismantle such a large number of warheads in relation to NATO forces under the proposed 'zero option'.

The SS–20 is deployed on a wheeled launcher with the missile housed in a launch tube which is elevated to the vertical prior to firing, and which can theoretically be used to launch further reload missiles. Some sources claim that every launch vehicle is allocated 2 missiles but this is not confirmed. Nine transporter-erector-launcher vehicles constitute a brigade and would be dispersed to pre-surveyed sites in time of tension. Some of these sites may be protected by earth revetments. The TEL has only limited cross-country ability and each group of 3 TELs is accompanied by several support vehicles including 2 large control and communications centres. The reaction time of the SS–20 is under one hour, a substantial improvement on the SS–4 and SS–5.

There are 441 SS–20 missiles deployed by the Soviet Union. At least 162 are based in Eastern Asia within range of Japan and China, but not Western Europe. The remainder are based within range of Western Europe with one group, possibly one-third of the total, based immediately east of the Urals within range of both Western Europe and South East Asia.

SS–X–28

This is a successor missile to the SS–20 and is being flight-tested. It is expected to be more acurrate and more easily land-mobile than the SS–20 and could be deployed before 1990. Most analysts assume that it will have a full MIRV system of warheads but one report suggests a single warhead system, though this seems unlikely. Early reports that the SS–X–28 might have a terminal-guidance system similar to the RADAG of the Pershing 2 have not been confirmed and may represent the origin of the idea that the SS–X–28 was a single-warhead missile.

SS–CX–4

Although the Soviet Union has had a ground-launched cruise missile, the SS–C–1B Sepal, in service for many years, this is a short-range anti-ship missile for coastal deployment. Reports of an intermediate-range GLCM surfaced in the early 1980s, and US DoD sources predicted a deployment of such missiles by 1985. By early 1987 the most reliable source indicated that flight-testing was continuing, with possible deployment before the end of the year.

The SS–CX–4 is reported to be broadly similar to the AS–15 in size and range, and it may be carried on a launcher taking 4 rounds but using similar operational procedures to the SS–20. It is unlikely to be deployed outside the Soviet Union, and may have a TERCOM-style guidance system in addition to inertial guidance.

Experimental GLCM

Unconfirmed reports suggest that a large GLCM, based on the SS–NX–24 may be under development, and might be capable of carrying a large warhead made up of conventional sub-munitions rather than a nuclear payload.

SS–NX–21

This missile is a submarine-launched version of the AS–15 and was expected to be deployed as early as 1984. Deployment had still not commenced in early 1987 but was reported to be imminent, with *Victor*, and modified *Yankee* submarines the most likely carriers. It can be fired from conventional torpedo tubes, much like the US Tomahawk, but its range is estimated at 1,850 miles, rather more than the Tomahawk. The SS–NX–21 could also be carried on new SSN boats such as the *Mike*, *Akula* and *Sierra* classes.

SS–NX–24

A large new submarine-launched cruise missile is under development which could enter service before the end of the decade. Trials are proceeding using a highly modified *Yankee* boat and it is not yet clear whether an entirely new class of submarine is under development. The SS–NX–24 is reported to be substantially larger than the SS–NX–21, with a length of just under 40 feet and a wingspan

of 19 feet. The missile is launched with wings retracted, presumably using a rocket-booster. Warhead-yield, range and missile accuracy are not known but it is reasonable to assume that such a large missile will have a substantially greater range than the SS–NX–21.

Tupolev Tu–16 (Badger)

This twin-jet subsonic medium bomber was the backbone of Soviet bomber forces in the 1960s and 1970s and has been exported to many countries. It is now being withdrawn from service in the bombing role as the Backfire takes over, but recent reports suggest that 285 remain operational with the air force in the strike role, together with naval aviation having a further 240. All are dual-capable and the number dedicated to a nuclear strike role may be much smaller than the overall total implies. The Tu–16 has a 4,000 mile range, a potential weapons load of 9 tons and can carry AS–4 and AS–6 stand-off missiles.

Tupolev Tu–22 (Blinder)

This supersonic medium-range twin-jet bomber was developed in the late 1950s, first deployed in 1962 and expected to be the mainstay of the Soviet nuclear forces in the medium-range category. The plane did not prove very successful which probably explains continued production of the Badger. Even so, 165 remain in service, 130 with the air force and the remainder in naval aviation. It has a range of 3,600 miles which can be extended by aerial refuelling. The Tu–22A carries free-fall bombs and the Tu–22B carries a single fuselage-mounted AS–4 missile.

Tupolev Tu–22M/Tu–26 (Backfire)

Originally considered a derivative of the Blinder (hence Tu–22M), the Backfire is recognised as a new aircraft type and a much more effective supersonic bomber than the Blinder. It has a range of up to 6,500 miles and can carry an 8-ton bomb load at just under Mach 2. It is a large swing-wing plane which could theoretically be used in a strategic role but is actually deployed as an effective intermediate and naval strike plane. Development took ten years and the plane was introduced in small numbers from 1974. Production built up to 30 per year by the early 1980s and there are now 260 in service, 140

with the air force and 120 in naval aviation. Two-thirds of the Backfires are deployed in the European Soviet Union. The Backfire can carry a wide range of conventional ordinance and also free-fall nuclear bombs. It can also carry a single fuselage-mounted AS–4 missile or 2 AS–4s on wing-base pylons. One recent report suggests that the usual range estimate of 6,500 miles is too great, and that actual range for combat missions is nearer 5,000 miles. This can be extended with aerial refuelling.

Naval Tactical Nuclear Weapons

The Soviet Union does not have nuclear-capable carrier-based aircraft and even when the first fleet-carrier enters service around 1990 this will probably deploy only STOVL aircraft rather than catapault-launched planes. Instead, the Soviet Navy has developed and deployed a much wider range of nuclear-tipped missiles than the US Navy, intended for anti-ship action but capable, in some instances, of being available for attacking coastal and even inland targets.

SS–N–3 (Shaddock)

This missile was first deployed in 1962 and is now being phased out. Numbers have decreased from around 300 to less than 240 over the three years to early 1987. It can be launched from submarines or surface ships, using different configurations and is deployed on *Juliet* and possibly *Whiskey* submarines, *Kynda* cruisers and *Kresta* destroyers. Its maximum range is 300 miles but its effective range, in terms of accuracy, is far less. The Shaddock can carry a 1,000-lb HE warhead or a 350-kiloton nuclear warhead. It is being replaced by the SS–N–12.

SS–N–7

The SS–N–7 is a 30-mile-range subsonic sea-skimming cruise missile which can be fired from *Charlie 1*-class nuclear submarines, each having 8 launch tubes. It is dual-capable, can carry a 200-kiloton warhead and could be used for coastal as well as anti-ship attack. It does not appear to have been a particular success and current numbers are below 80. Deployment commenced in 1968.

SS–N–9 (Siren)

The Siren is probably a development of the SS–N–7 and is deployed mainly on *Nanuchka* corvettes although probably on some submarines. Its operational range is reported to be 50 miles and it can carry a 200-kiloton warhead. It was first deployed in the late 1960s and current deployments are estimated at between 150 and 200.

SS–N–12 (Sandbox)

First deployed in 1973, this replacement for the SS–N–3 can use the same launchers. It has a maximum range of 350 miles at Mach 2.5, although unconfirmed reports claim a range of over 1,000 miles at transonic speeds. It is carried on *Kiev*-class carriers, *Slava*-class cruisers and *Echo*-class submarines. The carriers are equipped with reloads. The missile appears only to be deployed in the nuclear-armed form and carries a 350-kiloton warhead. There are 120 currently in service.

SS–N–14 (Silex)

This is broadly similar to the US ASROC missile and has been in service since 1974. It can dispense a homing torpedo or a low-kiloton-range nuclear depth-bomb at a range of up to 30 miles. There are 228 SS–N–14s deployed in both configurations — the number which are nuclear-tipped being unclear.

SS–N–15

Broadly similar to the US SUBROC, this is widely deployed with a low-kiloton-range nuclear warhead on six different classes of nuclear-powered submarine. It has a range of about 25 miles and perhaps 400 have been deployed. The *SS–N–16* is a broadly similar missile but probably carries a homing torpedo rather than a nuclear warhead.

SS–N–19 (Shipwreck)

This 300-mile-range Mach 2.5 missile entered service in 1980 and is deployed in vertical launch tubes on *Kirov*-class cruisers (20 tubes)

and *Oscar*-class cruise missile submarines (24 tubes). The 2 cruisers and 3 submarines collectively have 112 launch tubes with a similar number of missiles, as reloads are not carried. A 500-kiloton warhead can be carried but a high-explosive warhead may also be deployed. The SS–N–19 is primarily an anti-ship missile.

SS–N–22

This is a development of the SS–N–9 with a range increased to about 75 miles. It is probably dual-capable and can carry a 200-kiloton nuclear warhead. It is deployed on 6 *Sovremenny*-class cruisers (8 per ship) and is also carried on a trials corvette. Operational deployment stands at 48 missiles and it came into service in 1981. One source suggests a range of 250 miles but this has not been confirmed.

FRAS–1

This unguided anti-submarine rocket is carried on *Moskva*-class helicopter-carriers and *Kiev*-class aircraft-carriers. It has a range of around 20 miles, entered service in 1975 and carries a 5-kiloton nuclear depth-bomb. The launcher total is 10 but reloads may be carried.

Nuclear-armed Torpedoes and Sea Mines

The Soviet Navy deploys a wide range of torpedoes of many types, including nuclear-armed torpedoes for use against ports and naval bases. These are reported to have a yield of around 15 kilotons. A small number of nuclear-armed mines is also available, with yields reported to be in the 5 to 20 kiloton range.

Army Tactical Nuclear Weapons

The Soviet armed forces have long had three types of tactical ballistic missile, the FROG, Scud and Scaleboard, which cover a range from 40 to nearly 500 miles. The first two are now being replaced by SS–21 and SS–23 missiles respectively, and the Scaleboard is being deployed in a modified form. Estimates of dates of deployment and numbers in service of the new missiles have been

greatly exaggerated in Western circles in recent years.

FROG–7

A number of versions of the Free Rocket Over Ground (FROG) battlefield missile have been produced, and the FROG–7 is the last of the line, rather similar to the obsolete US Honest John. The FROG–7 was first deployed in 1965 but is progressively being replaced by the SS–21, less than 500 remaining in service in early 1987. It is carried on a wheeled launcher and is a spin-stabilised unguided artillery rocket with a range of up to 40 miles capable of carrying conventional or nuclear warheads, the latter being rated at 10, 20 or 200 kilotons. The FROG–7 has an accuracy of 1,300 feet CEP. A twin launcher has recently been reported.

SS–21

This FROG–7 replacement is broadly similar to the US Lance and was first deployed in 1978. Initial deployment rates were slow, suggesting possible development problems, and only 60 were in service by 1984. By early 1987 deployments had reached around 300, with 100 in the GDR and Czechoslovakia, but it is reported that the standard payload is conventional sub-munitions, although a 100-kiloton nuclear warhead can also be fitted. The 20-foot-long missile has a throw-weight of 1,000 lb over a 70 mile range and inertial guidance gives a CEP of 1,000 feet.

SS–1c (Scud B)

This 110-mile-range tactical ballistic missile has an inertial-guidance system giving an accuracy of 3,000 feet CEP with a nuclear warhead of up to 100 kilotons. Its range can be extended to over 200 miles with a conventional warhead and both versions are fired from a wheeled launcher. The Scud B is 34 feet long and has a launch-weight of 6 tons. Rather less than 400 remain in service but this includes conventional as well as nuclear versions. The replacement is the SS–23.

SS–12 (Scaleboard)

This is the largest of the trio of tactical ballistic missiles and is

sometimes categorised as a Shorter-range Intermediate Nuclear Force (SRINF) weapon. It entered service in 1969, has a range of 500 miles and an accuracy of 1,600 feet CEP, carrying an 800-kiloton nuclear warhead. Most have now been withdrawn from service in favour of the new SS–12M.

SS–12M (Scaleboard)

This missile was originally described as an entirely new missile, designated SS–22 and deployed first in 1979. It is now clear that it is no more than a modification to the SS–12 and the 'SS–22' designation has been dropped. The SS–12M carries a 1-megaton warhead and has a range of 550 miles with a CEP of 1,000 feet. Up to 130 are deployed, with some located in the GDR and Czechoslovakia. It is reported to be carried on a twin launcher.

SS–23 (Spider)

The SS–23 was originally reported as having been deployed in 1979, but it is now clear that it was only introduced in the mid-1980s. It has a range of around 310 miles and can carry a 100-kiloton warhead or conventional munitions. The Spider is launched from an 8-wheel launcher with a reload capability. Response time is much lower than the Scud, with a possible reload time of 30 minutes. In 1985 45 Spider launchers became operational with a brigade in the Belorussian Military District. Up to 250 were reported to be in service in early 1987 but these figures may be considerable overestimates. The accuracy of the Spider is variously reported in the range 1,200 to 1,500 feet. Some analysts suggest that it could provide an appropriate system for delivering sub-munitions, but the accuracy seems too low for this.

SA–5 (Gammon)

Although operated by the air defence forces, it is convenient to describe the SA–5 here. It is a long-range surface-to-air missile broadly similar to the US Nike-Hercules and fitted either with a high-explosive or low-kiloton nuclear warhead. It has a slant range of 150 miles, a maximum altitude of 100,000 feet and was introduced in 1967. Over 2,000 are in service, mainly in the conventional form, and the SA–5 is unlikely to be effective against low-flying bombers.

SA–10 (Growler)

Unconfirmed reports suggest that a nuclear-armed version of this modern anti-aircraft missile may be deployed. Growler has a range of up to 60 miles, and over 700 have been deployed in around 80 sites throughout the Soviet Union. It is reported to have a limited ability against cruise missiles in the conventionally-armed form.

Nuclear-capable Artillery

Until the end of the 1970s, there was little indication that the Soviet armed forces placed much reliance on nuclear-capable artillery, surface-to-surface missiles being the preferred way of deploying ground-based battlefield nuclear weapons. The one exception was the S–23 180 mm towed gun, capable of firing an AFAP over an 18 mile range.

Three new nuclear-capable artillery pieces have been added to the inventory, a 152 mm gun, a 203 mm gun and a 240 mm howitzer. The AFAPs are reported to have a yield of 2 to 5 kilotons. Together with older 152 mm howitzers which now appear to be able to fire AFAPs, the total number of nuclear-capable artillery pieces is approaching 10,000.

AFAP production appears to have been limited, and the number of artillery pieces actually designated dual-capable is probably a small part of the total. In 1985 it was reported that total deployments of AFAPs and air-delivered nuclear gravity bombs in the European theatre was 2,000, compared with some 4,100 for NATO.

Nuclear-capable Strike Aircraft

In addition to the intermediate-range aircraft, the Soviet Union deploys four types of nuclear-capable strike aircraft. Two further aircraft types have been deployed during the 1980s which may, in future, be used in a nuclear strike role.

Sukhoi Su–17 Fitter

The Su–7 Fitter A has now been virtually withdrawn from service but a number of the later SU–17 Fitter types remain widely deployed. The Fitter is a swing-wing ground attack fighter which

entered service in 1974 and can carry a weapons load of up to 5 tons. It has a combat radius of up to 425 miles (hi-lo-hi) and a maximum speed at height of Mach 2.1. Around 900 of all types are currently deployed.

MiG–21 Fishbed

A nuclear-capable version of this fighter was deployed in the early 1970s and around 130 remain in service. It has a combat radius of just over 300 miles with a small 2,000-lb weapons load, which could consist of a single bomb. Two nuclear bombs can be carried but over a more restricted range.

MiG–27 Flogger D/J

Two versions of this widely deployed plane were developed as ground attack aircraft. These versions of this swing-wing supersonic plane can carry a 3.5 ton weapon load over a 400 mile combat radius. Around 800 are deployed.

Sukhoi Su–24 Fencer

Analogous to the F–111, although it carries barely half that plane's weapons load, this large supersonic swing-wing attack aircraft was first deployed in 1974 and was produced in large numbers, perhaps 700 remaining in service. The combat radius of this Mach 2.3 plane is 1,100 miles.

Anti-Submarine Aircraft

The Soviet Union has three types of aircraft which can be equipped with an anti-submarine nuclear depth-bomb. These are the *Tu–142 Bear F*, the *Il–38 May* and the *Be–12 Mail*. About 200 of these aircraft are in service.

Future Strike Aircraft

Two new fighters have come into service in the interceptor role but may eventually be deployed, in later variants, as nuclear-capable strike aircraft.

Su–27 Flanker. Broadly similar to the US F–15, this appears to have had a troubled development. It first flew back in 1977, but of the 75 so far produced, very few are yet in squadron service.

MiG–29 Fulcrum. The Fulcrum entered service in October 1983 as an interceptor and variants of it are being exported. Production rates within the Soviet Union have been slower than expected, with 150 now operational.

Carrier-based Aircraft

It was originally expected that the construction of the Soviet Union's first fleet-carrier, the *Brezhnev*, would give the Soviet Union a greatly improved naval aviation force. It now appears that the carrier, due to commence trials before the end of the 1980s, will initially embark STOVL aircraft. These are unlikely to be nuclear-capable. Nuclear-capable carrier-based aircraft may yet be a decade away. A second carrier is under construction and 2 more are likely to be built by the year 2000.

United Kingdom

Britain exploded its first atom bomb in October 1952 and its first hydrogen bomb in May 1957. Until the late 1960s the RAF maintained Britain's strategic nuclear force and from 1969 this role was taken over by the Royal Navy's *Resolution*-class Polaris submarines.

Britain maintains a number of delivery systems for tactical nuclear weapons, most of them dual-capable. The weapons include bombs, depth-bombs, artillery shells and short-range missiles. Some are British-made but others are of US origin and are operated under a 'dual key' system.

Britain has a comprehensive nuclear weapons research and development programme, with overall responsibility vested in the Controller of R & D Establishment, Research and Nuclear (CERN) at the Ministry of Defence in Whitehall. The major R & D Centre is the Atomic Weapons Research Establishment at Aldermaston near Reading, Berkshire, which also undertakes some warhead production work. Two Royal Ordnance Factories, at Llanishen near Cardiff, and Burghfield in Berkshire, are also committed to the nuclear weapons programme and work closely with Aldermaston.

The AWRE employs some 5,000 people and had, in the mid-1980s, an annual budget of around £1,000 million. This is likely to rise as a major expansion programme is undergone at a cost approaching £400 million, centred on the building of the A90 warhead manufacturing facility which is initially concerned with Trident warhead manufacture.

The A90 plant was scheduled to commence Trident warhead production in 1986 and complete the 400 to 500 warheads by 1991. This is now well behind schedule and the Trident warhead programme may now take until 1995. According to US sources, the A90 plant does not have the capacity to produce Trident and tactical warheads simultaneously, so Britain's ageing WE177 tactical nuclear bomb will not be replaced until the mid-1990s.

While AWRE is the main R & D centre and is also concerned

with warhead production, the ROF at Llanishen also undertakes some early stages of the production of fissile and non-fissile components. ROF Burghfield employs some 600 people and is concerned with final assembly and initial storage. The most important civil contractors are Huntings and British Aerospace. Fuses for some warheads are produced by Greasby Electronics.

Strategic Nuclear Weapons

Polaris

In 1962, the Macmillan government committed Britain to the deployment of a quasi-independent strategic nuclear force based on the Polaris A–3 missile. Four *R*-class submarines were built, *Resolution, Renown, Repulse* and *Revenge*. Each is nuclear-powered, has a 7,500-ton displacement and carries 16 missiles in vertical launch tubes. The submarines are based at Faslane on the Lower Clyde, the associated weapons depot is at Coulport and major refits are undertaken at Rosyth. One submarine is normally in refit with 3 at Faslane. Of these, one is maintained on patrol in the Eastern Atlantic, a water space agreement with the United States delineating patrol areas. One submarine is normally working up for patrol or transiting the patrol area. A third is usually at Faslane. All 3 could be used in conflict — even the boat at Faslane has a reaction time of as little as 30 minutes in time of crisis. Each Polaris missile has a range of 2,500 miles and in its original warhead configuration, delivered 3 200-kiloton thermonuclear warheads in an MRV system with aim points 9 miles apart in a triangular pattern. The missile was thus intended for use against large dispersed urban-industrial targets.

A major development programme to upgrade the Polaris warheads was instituted in the early 1970s resulting in a new 'front-end' for the missile termed Chevaline, intended to counter the Moscow-based Galosh ABM system and its successors. The precise configuration has not been made public but appears to involve maneouvring the missile front-end prior to warhead/decoy release to confuse Soviet missile defence radar. The weight penalty involved in this system results in a smaller throw-weight, and the configuration appears to be 3 50-kiloton warheads. These are also dispersed in an essentially MRV rather than MIRV system although the MRV spread pattern may be varied.

A mid-term cost estimate for Chevaline was £1,000 million at 1980 prices, but, as well as inflation, there have been considerable development problems and cost over-runs, and unofficial estimates now exceed £2,000 million. It was originally due to be deployed in 1979 but was delayed until 1983 when *Revenge* went operational with Chevaline. All 4 boats will have been retrofitted with Chevaline by 1988.

Because of problems of deterioration, the solid-fuel rocket-motors of the entire Polaris missile inventory were replaced between 1982 and 1986 at a cost of £370 million. Even so, major problems of reliability continue. Of the 12 missile tests conducted between 1985 and 1987, 3 failed. A 25 per cent failure rate for experimental missiles would cause concern. Such a failure rate for operational strategic missiles is highly unusual.

Trident

On 11 July 1980, the UK government announced it would purchase the Lockheed Trident C4 SLBM to fit to British-built SSBN to replace Polaris. The 8-MIRV system would replace the Polaris MRV, representing an eight-fold increase in targeting capability. The Trident C4 order was transferred to the more advanced D5 missile in March 1982, with submarines and warheads produced in Britain and missiles, guidance and MIRV bus produced in the US.

Trident D5 could carry a 17-MIRV system but SALT II limits specify an SLBM MIRV maximum of 14. The UK government has stated that it plans up to an 8-MIRV system, below the missile's full capability but allowing a greater range. A higher warhead allocation could follow improvements to Moscow's ABM defences. Trident D5 is far more accurate than Polaris, with a 400 feet CEP probable.

Like Polaris, Trident will be fully integrated into NATO nuclear targeting which is, in turn, done in collaboration with US strategic targeting. The UK force *could* be used independently, and the missile submarines do carry targeting tapes for their missile fire control systems prepared by UK as well as NATO officials.

The first Trident SSBN, HMS *Vanguard* was ordered in April 1986 and others of the *Vanguard* class will be *Vengeance*, *Victorious*, and *Venerable*. Each will have a submerged displacement of 15,500 tons, a length of almost 500 feet, a 42-foot beam and will carry 16 launch tubes. Each boat will cost £1000 million excluding missiles and warheads. Main contractor is Vickers of Barrow, and Rolls-Royce will

produce the reactor. *Vanguard* will enter service in the mid-1990s.

Tactical Nuclear Weapons

The British Army, Air Force and Navy all have a number of tactical nuclear weapons systems. Britain produces free-fall bombs but not AFAPs or tactical missile warheads although this was considered in the 1950s.

Lance

The British Army of the Rhine has one regiment of 4 batteries equipped with 12 launchers, and also reload vehicles, for the Lance tactical nuclear missile. The total number of missiles is estimated at 84 with the W70 warheads held in US custody (see US entry for warhead details). The Mod 3 enhanced radiation (neutron) version of the W70 is stored in the US and the UK government has not indicated that it would be deployed with the BAOR.

M109

This 155 mm (6 inch) howitzer is a 24-ton self-propelled vehicle which can fire the US W48 AFAP with a yield of 0.1 kilotons at the rate of 4 shells a minute. Until early 1981, the army had 50 M109s equipping 4 artillery regiments of the BAOR, but a further 69 were purchased in 1981–3. Some older models have been withdrawn and 101 are currently in service.

M110

This larger 28-ton self-propelled howitzer is also of American manufacture and fires 203 mm (8 inch) shells. It is nuclear-capable and can fire the US W33 shell with a yield of up to 12 kilotons. The M110 has a range of 19 miles and would be capable of taking the US/W79 AFAP which will be neutron-capable. The BAOR has 16 M110s in North Germany.

FH–70 and SP–70

Two new howitzers were under development for Britain, France and Germany in the early 1980s, the FH–70 towed howitzer and the SP–70 self-propelled howitzer. After protracted development problems, the SP–70 was cancelled in January 1987, but the FH–70 has been widely deployed, with 72 in service with the British Army.

The FH–70 is not currently deployed in a nuclear-capable role and any AFAP would have to be produced by the United States. Unconfirmed reports in mid-1983 suggested that a request for an AFAP for the FH–70 and SP–70 had been put by some European governments to the United States government. With the collapse of the SP–70 programme, however, it is likely that the nuclear-capable M109 will be purchased in its place, and the FH–70 will remain in a conventional role.

Atomic Demolition Munitions

Personnel within the BAOR have been trained in the emplacement of ADMs but these munitions are not now stored in Europe for NATO use. They appear now to be restricted to US Special Forces, although these units could use them in Europe.

Buccaneer

The Hawker Siddeley Buccaneer is the oldest nuclear-capable strike aircraft still in service with the RAF. It has been withdrawn from front-line service with RAF Germany and is now deployed in the maritime strike role at Lossiemouth in Scotland with 12 and 208 squadrons. Of 52 aircraft, 18 are in reserve, but the remainder are undergoing a limited life extension programme for service into the mid-1990s. The Buccaneer is regarded as a rugged aircraft and has a combat radius of up to 1,100 miles.

Jaguar

The Jaguar is a single-seat nuclear-capable strike aircraft which can deliver kiloton-range nuclear bombs over a 1,000 mile combat radius when equipped with external fuel tanks. Of the 75 Sepecat Jaguars remaining in service, 36 of them are in the FGA/close support role. Planes replaced by Tornadoes in West Germany have

been used to augment squadrons in the UK. It is reported, however, that Jaguars are currently deployed solely in a conventional role.

Tornado

The Tornado programme is Britain's most expensive aircraft programme and has been developed in strike (GRI) and interceptor (F2/3) versions by the Anglo-German-Italian Panavia consortium. There are 229 GRI nuclear-capable Tornadoes entering RAF service, equipping 11 squadrons, 8 of them in West Germany. Around 200 were already in service by early 1987, but, with an attrition buy, the final number may well be around 270 at a cost well in excess of £6,000 million.

The Tornado has a combat radius of over 800 miles in hi-lo-lo-hi mode, but this would routinely be extended considerably by aerial refuelling. It has also been reported that additional conformal fuel tanks are being fitted to UK-based Tornadoes. The plane has true all-weather ability and its terrain-following navigation system allows low-level penetration of air space and the navigation attack system allows single-pass attacks on targets.

With the transfer of 9 squadrons from Honington in Suffolk to Bruggen in West Germany in October 1986, 7 squadrons had been formed in West Germany and 2 in Britain. The Tornado carries the British-made WE177 free-fall nuclear bomb but the RAF is seeking a new weapon, preferably a stand-off missile. One possibility would be a nuclear-armed 500-mile-range version of the Sea Eagle, and another would be for the UK to produce a nuclear-armed version of the non-nuclear Modular Stand-Off Weapon (MSOW), currently planned by 7 NATO countries. In April 1987 it was reliably reported that the UK Ministry of Defence was engaged in discussions with French authorities on purchasing up to 100 ASMP missiles at £4 million each, these to be fitted with a variant of the Trident nuclear warhead.

Harrier

The current Harrier GR3 is not nuclear-capable but its replacement, the GR5, will be. From late 1988 102 aircraft will enter service, the major part of the force forming 2 large squadrons at RAF Gutersloh. This versatile STOVL plane will be employed in the ground attack role and the Ministry of Defence has stated that it

will not be deployed in a nuclear role. However, it was reported in May 1987 that the RAF was intent on deploying it in a nuclear strike role. Deliveries commenced in July 1987.

Advanced Harrier

British Aerospace worked in the early 1980s on a project to produce a Mach 2 STOVL successor to the Harrier GR5. The project was curtailed in late 1982 in favour of the international European Fighter Aircraft (EFA) project, but problems with that aircraft could lead to a renewed interest in the P–1216 design. The main advantage would be the versatility of deployment without reliance on runways, but funds are not currently available from UK sources for further developments. It is possible that British Aerospace could link with McDonnell-Douglas in further development of the programme as the US Marine Corps has expressed an interest in the project. While any such plane would be primarily an interceptor, ground attack functions would be likely to involve a nuclear capability.

Nimrod

The British Aerospace Nimrod MR2 maritime reconnaissance/anti-submarine warfare aircraft operates out of St Mawgan in Cornwall (1 squadron) and Kinloss in Moray (3 squadrons). One of its major roles is ASW, and munitions include the US B–57 nuclear depth-bomb, operated under dual control. Stocks are maintained at St Mawgan and Macrihanish. Nimrod MR2s in service total 31, all in the MR/ASW role.

Sea Harrier

The British Aerospace Sea Harrier STOVL strike aircraft operates from 3 Royal Navy carriers and can deliver the WE177 free-fall nuclear bomb. The plane could undertake attacks on major surface ships and, conceivably, land targets — toss-bombing techniques would allow the Harrier to release its nuclear ordnance up to 7 miles from the target. The navy has 26 Sea Harriers, 3 of which are trainers, and a further 23 are on order. A mid-life update of 30 FRS MRI Sea Harriers to FRS 2 standard is underway, with the first due to fly in February 1988. Sea Harriers equip 3 squadrons, 2 of which

are carrier-based and the other at RNAS Yeovilton in Somerset.

Helicopters

All of the Royal Navy's ASW helicopters are nuclear-capable and can deliver a depth-bomb ASW version of the WE177. The major components of the force are 61 Sea King HAS–2/–5 helicopters, operating from carriers and shore bases, and 75 Lynx HAS–2/–3 operating from up to 46 destroyers and frigates. Ships of the *Invincible* and *Broadsword* classes are authorised to carry nuclear weapons in peacetime, others would be restricted to wartime deployments. The Sea King can carry 4 WE177s and the Lynx 2. The Sea King HAS–5 is being upgraded to HAS–6 by avionics improvements, including a new MAD. The eventual successor to the Sea King will be the Anglo-Italian Westland-Agusta EH–101. The project is well behind schedule and will not enter service until the mid-1990s.

Nuclear Warheads

Most UK nuclear delivery systems have warheads which are either US produced or based closely on US designs. An exception is the Chevaline warhead which appears to be indigenous, as does the Trident warhead, reported to have a 150-kiloton-yield. UK-built tactical nuclear warheads have been of two types, a 600 lb lightweight warhead and a 950 lb medium warhead, the latter having a yield of up to 1 megaton. The medium warhead appears to have been withdrawn from service in the early 1980s.

The WE177 lightweight warhead is based on the US B57 design and is available in two configurations, ground/air burst for land and maritime strike, and depth-bomb for anti-submarine warfare. It is reported to be a variable-yield device with a range of between 5 and 200 kilotons, although the depth-bomb variant would be at the lower end of this range. The number of warheads in the UK stockpile is a matter of some controversy. Most sources have suggested a range of between 200 and 500 tactical nuclear weapons, excluding US-controlled warheads. More recent sources indicate a far lower figure, possibly no more than 125 WE177 warheads, with just 25 of these in the depth-bomb configuration. This latter figure is probably more accurate.

The long delays with the Trident warhead programme mean that the production of new tactical nuclear weapons for air force and

navy use will be delayed until well into the 1990s, and stocks of the WE177 will then be up to thirty years old and may well have been subject to substantial deterioration. A partial solution will be to modify Trident warheads for fitting to a stand-off missile such as the ASMP, and to extend the production run of the Trident warheads. This will not, however, resolve the problem of a future requirement for nuclear depth-bombs for the navy.

Table 5 Basing of RAF nuclear-capable aircraft[a] — June 1987

Squadron	Aircraft	Base
6	Jaguar	Coltishall, Norfolk
9	Tornado	Bruggen, West Germany
12	Buccaneer	Lossiemouth, Grampian
14	Tornado	Bruggen, West Germany
15	Tornado	Laarbruch, West Germany
16	Tornado	Laarbruch, West Germany
17	Tornado	Bruggen, West Germany
20	Tornado	Laarbruch, West Germany
27	Tornado	Marham, Norfolk
31	Tornado	Bruggen, West Germany
38[b]	Nimrod	St Mawgan, Cornwall
42	Nimrod	St Mawgan, Cornwall
45[b]	Tornado	Honington, Suffolk
54	Jaguar	Coltishall, Norfolk
120	Nimrod	Kinloss, Grampian
201	Nimrod	Kinloss, Grampian
206	Nimrod	Kinloss, Grampian
208	Buccaneer	Lossiemouth, Moray
617	Tornado	Marham, Norfolk

Note: a Includes Jaguars currently deployed solely in a conventional role.
b Shadow squadron designation for conversion unit

France

France began to develop its own nuclear weapons soon after the end of the Second World War and conducted its first atom bomb test near Reggan in the Sahara on 13 February 1960, thus becoming the world's fourth nuclear power. After the failure of attempts to gain US help in the development of nuclear delivery systems, France proceeded to develop its own forces. The first of these was the Mirage IVA nuclear bomber, some of which remain in service. This was followed by land-launched and submarine-launched ballistic missiles (SSBS – *Sol-sol-balistique stratégique* — and MSBS — *Mer-sol balistique stratégique*).

Thus France maintains, on a small scale, a triad of nuclear delivery systems analogous to those of the United States and the Soviet Union. It also has a small arsenal of tactical nuclear weapons. The heavy French commitment to indigenous nuclear weapons and delivery systems has meant that 12 to 20 per cent of the French defence budget over the past twenty years has gone on nuclear forces, perhaps twice that of the United Kingdom. This has imposed a strain on other programmes and has meant, for example, that France has not developed a significant fleet of nuclear-powered attack submarines. There are at present just 2 in service and 4 on order.

Although France is not formally integrated into the military command structure of NATO, it remains a signatory of the North Atlantic Alliance, and informal links between France and other signatories are close. France bases 50,000 troops, including 3 armoured divisions in West Germany, and a force of 2,700 in West Berlin. The French government is committed to maintaining defence expenditure with a particular emphasis on nuclear forces. France is opposed to the inclusion of UK and French nuclear forces in arms control negotiations in the forseeable future.

Land-based Missiles

SSBS S–3

The first land-based intermediate range missile, the S–2, was deployed from 1971 to 1982 when the second of 2 squadrons of 9 missiles was replaced with the S–3. It is produced by Aerospatiale and is a 2-stage inertially-guided solid-fuel missile with a range of 2,000 miles, able to reach any part of the European Soviet Union. Each missile is 48 feet long and 5 feet in diameter. It retains the first stage of the S–2 but has a more advanced second stage and a more heavily hardened re-entry vehicle equipped with penetration aids.

The S–3 has a substantially larger thermonuclear warhead than the S–2, rated at 1.2 megatons (compared with 150 kilotons for the S–2). It was first test-fired in December 1976 and the full sequence of development firings was completed within three years. The 2 squadrons of missiles are located at the Saint-Christol base on the Plateau d'Albion in Haute Provence and are housed in underground silos spaced up to 5 miles apart.

SSBS S–4

It is expected that future Soviet IRBMs such as the SS–28 will render the S–3 vulnerable, even though it is silo-based. Consequently, a new mobile IRBM, the S–4, is under development which is also intended to replace the Mirage IVA strategic bomber.

The S–4 missile is expected to be housed routinely in silos but will be dispersed in road-mobile vehicles on ordinary roads in time of crisis. It will be a solid-propellant 2-stage missile weighing around 10 tons and with a range of just under 3,000 miles. It will utilise M–4 technology, including guidance and possibly warheads. It was originally expected to have a single 150-kiloton warhead, with around 100 being deployed. Current plans appear to envisage just 33 missiles with each carrying a 3-MIRV system. Production may commence by 1990 with an IOC of 1996.

Submarine-launched Ballistic Missiles

The French SLBM force currently has 6 boats, 5 of them carrying the M–20 missile and 1 the M–4. A seventh is under construction,

the second of 2 boats of an interim class between 5 initial boats and a new class planned for the 1990s. Four of the original 5 boats will be retrofitted with the M–4 missile by 1990, with only *Le Redoutable* retaining the M–20. Provided the force of 7 boats available from 1990 proves capable of maintaining 3 boats on patrol at all times, *Le Redoutable* will be retired to a training role in the mid-1990s as the first of the new class is deployed. France also has a conventionally powered missile testing submarine, *Gymnote*, completed in 1966 but now in reserve.

Table 6 Specifications of the French SSBN fleet

Name	Designation	Laid down	Commissioned	Fitted with M–4
Le Redoutable	S611	Nov. 1964	Dec. 1971	—
Le Terrible	S612	Jun. 1967	Dec. 1973	1989
Le Foudroyant	S610	Dec. 1969	Jun. 1974	1990
L'Indomptable	S613	Dec. 1971	Jun. 1976	1988
Le Tonnant	S614	Oct. 1974	Apr. 1980	1987
L'Inflexible	S615	Mar. 1980	Jan. 1985	1985
	S616	1988	1994	1994

MSBS M–20

Four of the French SSBN still carry the M–20 missile with *Le Tonnant* retrofitting during 1987. The 2-stage solid-fuel missile is 34 feet long and weighs 20 tons. It has a range of 1,800 miles and a 2-stage burn-time of 1 minute 42 seconds. It carries a single 1-megaton warhead and is equipped with penetration aids.

MSBS M–4

This 3-stage solid-fuel SLBM is nearly twice the weight of the M–20 and carries a MIRV system of 6 150-kiloton warheads over a range of 2,500 miles. It was first test-fired in the Pacific in 1980 and was deployed on *L'Inflexible* in February 1985. It was originally reported that the M–4 had an MRV rather than an MIRV system, but more recent reports indicate that it can, at the least, vary its target spread over a rectangular area measuring about 210 by 100 miles.

The warheads fitted to M–4 missiles on *L'Inflexible* are of the TN

70 type, but *Le Tonnant* will carry missiles with TN 71 warheads, miniaturised versions of the TN 70, their lighter weight giving the missiles a range of 3,100 miles.

MSBS M–5

This is a follow-on to the M–4 and was previously designated M–4C. It will be fitted to the new class of SSBN due to be laid down in 1988 and commissioned in 1994. This 15,000-ton boat will have a greater diving depth but, despite its large size, will probably only carry 16 missile launch tubes. The M–5 will probably be substantially larger than the M–4, with a longer range and a 10- or 12-MIRV payload.

Prior to the commissioning of the new SSBN in 1994, the French SSBN fleet will therefore have 1 M–20 equipped boat delivering 16 warheads and 5 M–4 equipped boats delivering 96 warheads each. The total targeting capability will therefore be 496 compared with 80 in 1984.

Long-range Bombers and Associated Missiles

Dassault Mirage IVA/IVP

The Mirage IVA is a relatively small supersonic bomber which first flew in 1959. It was the foundation of French nuclear weapons strategy until the IRBMs and SLBMs were deployed in the early 1970s and was normally fitted with a single AN–22 free-fall nuclear bomb rated at 60 or 70 kilotons. Until early 1986, 34 planes were organised in 6 squadrons, with 6 planes in reserve. All but 18 will be phased out as the Mirage 2000N come into service from 1988. The remaining 18 were fitted with the ASMP stand-off cruise missile during 1986 and are currently organised into 2 squadrons at Marsan and Cazeux air-bases.

Retrofitting of the Mirage IVA with the ASMP (resulting in the IVP designation) was originally regarded as an interim measure, pending the deployment of the Mirage 2000N. This plane is intended for a tactical nuclear role and it was therefore decided to retain the 2 squadrons of the Mirage IVP until the deployment of the S–4 mobile IRBM in the mid-1990s.

ASMP (Air-sol a moyenne portée)

The ASMP is broadly similar to the SRAM stand-off missile built by Boeing, and is the result of a programme initiated in 1978 by Aerospatiale. It is a wingless cruise missile powered by a ram-jet motor using an initial rocket-booster after launch. It is about 16 feet long and has a launch-weight of 2,000 lb and is normally carried on a centre-line pylon, 1 per plane.

The ASMP carries a 150-kiloton warhead and has a high-altitute range of 150 miles at Mach 3 and a low-altitude terrain-following range of 50 miles at Mach 2. A total of 130 missiles is likely to be procured, mostly for Super Etendard and Mirage 2000N aircraft.

Tactical Nuclear Weapons

France has a variety of air- and ground-launched tactical nuclear weapons and the necessary delivery systems. All are being upgraded by the early 1990s.

The Tactical Air Force has 5 nuclear-capable strike squadrons, 3 equipped with 45 *Jaguars* and 2 with 30 *Mirage IIIEs*. All can carry the AN–52 15-kiloton free-fall nuclear bomb. The squadrons are to be re-equipped with 75 Mirage 2000N strike aircraft carrying the ASMP.

The French Naval Air Force has 3 strike squadrons equipped with 37 *Super Etendard* nuclear-capable aircraft which also carry the AN–52. Commencing in 1988, 24 of the aircraft will be retrofitted with the ASMP, operating from the carriers *Foch* and *Clemenceau*. They will remain in service until around the year 2000, or possibly 2005, but will eventually be replaced by the *Dassault Rafale B* which is expected to be nuclear-capable.

The 2 carriers will eventually be replaced by 2 nuclear-powered aircraft-carriers, the first of which, *Richelieu*, was ordered early in 1986. The 40,000-ton carrier will deploy 40 planes and will be commissioned in 1996.

Dassault Mirage 2000N

The Mirage 2000 was initially selected in 1975 as a fighter but it has evolved into a multi-role plane with the 2000N as a major derivative intended as a nuclear-capable strike aircraft replacing the Mirage

IIIEs and Jaguars currently fulfilling the tactical nuclear role for the air force.

The Mirage 2000N is a 2-seat supersonic low-altitude all-weather bomber. It has a strengthened airframe allowing it to fly at speeds of just under Mach 1 at low altitude (2,000 feet) employing the ESD/Thomson–CSF Antilope radar for navigation and terrain-following. The first of 2 prototypes flew for the first time in February 1983 and the first production model was delivered four years later in February 1987. An initial force of 36 aircraft is planned, rising eventually to 85. Squadron service starts in 1988.

Pluton

France does not at present have nuclear-capable artillery, but it does have a tactical surface-to-surface missile, the Pluton, which was first deployed in 1974 as a replacement for the US Honest John missile then in service with the French Army. The original production run was 120, but only 44 remain in service. It is launched from a mobile platform based on a tank chassis and has a range of up to 75 miles carrying a single warhead in the 10- to 15-kiloton range, although some sources suggest that a 25-kiloton derivative of the AN–52 can be carried. CEP is between 500 and 1,000 feet depending on range.

Hades

The development programme for this Pluton replacement was approved in 1981, with flight trials expected to commence in 1988 and initial deployment scheduled for 1992. Hades will have a maximum range of over 200 miles carrying a 10- to 25-kiloton warhead. It will be carried on a specially developed wheeled launcher, each of which will have a reload and carry 2 vertically launched missiles. While the launcher will not have the cross-country mobility of the Pluton, it will have a much greater speed and range. There are to be 180 missiles procured to equip 3 or 4 army regiments. Early reports that Hades would be air-breathing appear incorrect and it is reported to be a rocket-powered ballistic missile.

Enhanced Radiaton Weapon

An ER (neutron) warhead has been under development since the late 1970s and in July 1983 President Mitterrand confirmed that

France had the capacity to mass-produce the weapon but had not yet taken the decision to do so. In December 1986, the Defence Minister, André Giraud, indicated that production had commenced. An ER warhead could be used in a free-fall bomb but the most likely delivery method would be the Hades missile. Hades has been designed to be compatible with an ER warhead and in mid-1985 the French Army Chief of Staff reported that this would be the primary function of the Hades.

China

The first Chinese nuclear weapon test was on 16 October 1964 and was a tower-mounted uranium–235 device with a yield of 20 kilotons. In May 1965, China successfully tested an air-dropped device, a 30-kiloton weapon released from a modified Tupolev TU–4 bomber. The first test of a thermonuclear device, also air-dropped, came on 17 June 1967 and was rated at 3 megatons.

The early development of nuclear weapons by China involved considerable technical assistance from the Soviet Union, but from the early 1960s China continued its programme with little help. Most of the 30 or so nuclear weapon tests were in the 1970s, with 4 in 1976 alone. While a few have been underground, most have been air-dropped. No tests were reported from 1980 to 1983 and recent tests have tended to be conducted underground.

China is one of four countries, along with the United States, the Soviet Union and France, to have developed a strategic triad of weapons systems. It places relatively little reliance on tactical nuclear weapons but this may be increasing. Its defence policy towards the Soviet Union is one of nuclear deterrence against nuclear attack coupled with militia-style resistance to conventional attack. Its very large conventional forces result in over 25 per cent of Soviet conventional forces being assigned to the areas of Soviet Asia adjacent to China, a factor frequently left out of assessments of the NATO–Warsaw Pact military balance.

The annual production of nuclear weapons may be as high as 75, and estimates of the total size of the Chinese nuclear arsenal range from between 600 and 1,250. Forces are deployed in a manner to diminish the risk of a counter-force attack by the Soviet Union. This view is supported by an assessment published in the US Joint Chiefs of Staff Military Posture Statement for 1981 which states:

> China possesses a relatively small and comparatively unsophisticated force, which, nevertheless, serves as a credible nuclear deterrent to the Soviet Union. An innovative deployment strategy poses severe targeting

> problems for any potential aggressor. Survivability of some portion of the ballistic missile force is virtually guaranteed through launch unit mobility, hardened storage of launchers, concealment practices and dispersal in mountainous terrain. If the Soviets launched a nuclear attack on China, they would do so knowing that they would suffer significant damage in retaliation.

The deployment of the MIRVed SS–20 IRBM, the development of its more accurate replacement, the SS–X–28, improvements in remote sensing and target acquisition and the decrease in the reaction time of Soviet missiles all tend to diminish the credibility of this assessment. On the other hand, in 1981 China did not have the submarine-launched leg of the nuclear triad, and this development probably enhances the survivability of a portion of Chinese strategic forces after a counter-force attack.

Chinese nuclear forces present an increasing threat to the Soviet Union, the more so as China increases its military and technical links with Western countries. Technical cooperation from Western Europe has been in existence since 1973 and from the United States since 1978. Probably the most notable example of cooperation is the use by the United States of missile-tracking facilities in north-west China, an especially valuable resource in terms of gathering data on Soviet missile test-flights since the loss of such facilities in Iran.

While China is not a party to any major nuclear arms control negotiations, it became apparent in 1983 that China would be willing to participate in negotiations provided the United States and the Soviet Union were prepared to take a lead. A commitment by China to halve its nuclear arsenals would apparently follow a similar commitment by the superpowers. China maintains good relations with Pakistan and these appear to extend to assistance with Pakistan's nuclear weapons programme.

Land-based Missiles

CSS–1 (Chinese designation T–1)

This is China's oldest nuclear-armed ballistic missile and was first test-fired in 1966 and deployed around 1970. At least 50 and possibly as many as 100 remain deployed in North West China, each carrying a single 15- to 20-kiloton warhead. Reports that it has been retrofitted with a thermonuclear megaton-range warhead have not

been confirmed. The CSS–1 is a single-stage liquid-propellant MRBM, similar to, but more primitive than, the Soviet SS–4. It has been tested over a range of around 1,200 miles but its operational range is probably 1,000 miles.

CSS–2 (T–2)

This is a much more substantial IRBM probably based loosely on the Soviet SS–5 and first deployed in 1970. It is a single-stage storable liquid-fuel missile with a 1- to 3-megaton warhead and a range of up to 2,000 miles. Deployment of 60 to 70 in the early 1980s was accompanied by a continuing annual production of 5 missiles, and it is now estimated that around 100 are deployed. Like the CSS–1 it is deployed in North West China and its range enables it to reach all of the Soviet Union east of the Urals. The number of launch-sites for the CSS–2 appears to be greater than the number of missiles and it appears that the missile is readily transportable. Thus mobility rather than launch-site hardening is the basis of survivability.

CSS–3 (T–3)

This appears to have been an early attempt to produce a full-range ICBM by adding a second stage to the CSS–2 design. It was not fully successful and the missile's range is estimated at slightly over 4,000 miles, enabling it to reach European parts of the Soviet Union but not the United States (apart from Alaska). The CSS–3 was probably an interim solution pending the development of an entirely new ICBM. It is fuelled by storable liquid propellants and is silo-based. It probably carries a similar warhead to the CSS–2, between 1 and 3 megatons, and just 8 have been produced and deployed, although one recent and unsubstantiated report suggests a high annual production rate and a current deployment of 100 missiles.

CSS–4

This is a full-range ICBM capable of reaching any part of Europe or North America and is probably based on the Soviet SS–9 liquid-fuelled ICBM. Development commenced in 1970 but the first flight test was not until May 1980. It was tested twice that month over a 4,000 mile range but probably has an operational range of 8,000

miles. With a payload of some 2,500 lb it can carry a 5-megaton warhead. Deployment commenced in 1983 but, as of 1987, only 5 were in service, all silo-based. It appears that if production is continuing, then it is at a very slow rate, and resources may have been diverted into the CSS–5. It was reported in September 1985 that a new version of the CSS–4 had been flight-tested from Xichang in south-west China and that this version was fitted with a MIRV warhead system.

CSS–5

A new 3-stage ICBM, based on the Long March 3 satellite launcher, was first test-fired in 1984 and is now being deployed in small numbers. It probably exceeds the range of the CSS–4 and is only slightly smaller than the Soviet SS–18. It is probably equipped with a MIRV warhead system carrying up to 10 warheads.

Submarine-launched Ballistic Missiles

CSS–N–3

China's first operational SLBM is broadly similar to an early Polaris missile. It is 32 feet long and is a 2-stage missile developed from the CSS–2 IRBM. China commenced developing SLBM and SSBN in the mid-1970s having acquired a single *Golf*-class SSB with 3 launch tubes in the mid-1960s. This was built under licence from the Soviet Union at Dairen and the 3 missile tubes in its enlarged conning tower were subsequently converted to 2 tubes for test purposes. This SSB was not deployed operationally.

The first test-flight of a CSS–N–3 took place from a submerged pontoon at Huludao on 30 April 1982 and a second launch was conducted from the *Golf* SSB on 12 October of that year.

These details do, however, conflict with persistent reports in the autumn of 1981 that an experimental missile submarine had been lost with all crew in August 1981 when the rocket-motor of a missile being test-fired accidentally exhausted into the submarine's interior.

China developed the *Han* class of SSN in the early 1970s and commenced building *Xia*-class SSBN in 1978, with the first boat being launched in 1981. There are now 2 in service with at least 2

more under construction. A class of 7 boats is anticipated, each having a displacement of 8,000 tons and carrying 12 missile launch tubes. Later variants may have 16 tubes.

The range of the CSS–N–3 is variously estimated at 1,700 to 2,100 miles and the SSBN would patrol in the western Pacific and the South China Sea, giving a target coverage of the eastern USSR. Patrols in the India Ocean are possible which would extend the target coverage to the western Soviet Union. The missile carries a warhead estimated variously at between 20 kilotons and 2 megatons, precise details being unclear.

CSS–NX–4

A further SLBM is reported to be under development which is likely to have a longer range and to carry a single 2-megaton warhead.

Bombers

Xian Hong–6

This is the main Chinese nuclear-capable bomber and is closely based on the Tupolev Tu–16 Badger design. It is a large subsonic bomber with a range of just under 4,000 miles. Production continues at a slow annual rate at the Xian State Aircraft Factory. No more than 150 are in service and they are able to carry a single 1-megaton thermonuclear free-fall bomb. The Hong–6 has been used in at least 7 nuclear weapon tests and entered service in 1968. It has only a limited ability to penetrate Soviet air space.

Harbin Hong–5

This 1,350-mile-range light bomber is analogous to the British Canberra and is an old design based on the Soviet Il–28 Beagle. Production continues, slowly, at the Harbin State Aircraft Factory, but may now be limited to replacement of attrition losses. Over 600 Hong–5s remain in service, but over 150 of these are with naval aviation, and an unknown proportion of the air force planes will have a nuclear strike role. Most are probably intended for conventional bombing and reconnaissance functions.

Xian Hong–7

It is reported that China is developing a new version of the B–6 bomber with supersonic dash capability. It may parallel a more comprehensive programme to produce an entirely new indigenous supersonic nuclear bomber.

Tactical Nuclear Weapons

Information on China's tactical nuclear forces is sparse and should be treated with some caution. It is likely, however, that they include small free-fall nuclear bombs for strike aircraft, warheads for an unguided artillery missile and possibly a mine.

Nanchang Q–5

This is a substantially modified version of the Soviet twin-jet MiG–19 strike aircraft. It is being produced at the rate of at least 20 a year and over 300 are in service, foreign buyers including Pakistan and North Korea. It is a single-seat supersonic aircraft with a range, in hi-lo-hi format, of some 700 miles. It is a versatile aircraft capable of carrying a range of ordnance including a free-fall nuclear bomb rated at between a 5- and 20-kiloton yield.

T–5

It is reported that a 65-mile-range unguided artillery rocket has been deployed which is nuclear-capable. An unconfirmed report suggests that 150 have been deployed.

Artillery

Unconfirmed reports suggest that China has 180 mm or 203 mm artillery. If the former, it would be a towed weapon based on the Soviet S–23 howitzer. It is not clear whether China has actually developed AFAPs for other classes of weapon, although an unconfirmed report in 1986 suggested a stockpile of up to 100 weapons.

Mines

It has been suggested that China has produced a limited number of high-yield nuclear land-mines which could be pre-positioned on likely invasion routes. The tactic would be to allow initial formations of invading troops to pass the location of a mine, presumably in a mountain pass, and then detonate the device isolating the forces from the main invasion force. The development of such devices has not been confirmed.

Israel

Israel has never publicly confirmed its possession of nuclear weapons but is generally assumed to have had them for over 15 years. In 1974, President Katzir announced that Israel 'has the potential' to make a nuclear weapon, 'and if we need it, we will do it'. Israel has long maintained, however, that it would not be the first country to introduce weapons into the Middle East. These aims are not mutually exclusive as the United States, the Soviet Union, Britain and France have all based tactical nuclear weapons in the Middle East.

A reasonably authoritative early report of Israel's nuclear capability came from William Beecher in the *Boston Globe* in 1975, stating that Israel then had 10 atomic weapons. Mr Beecher had previously been Deputy Assistant Secretary for Defence (Public Affairs) in the US Government for two years.

In the early 1980s, there were reports that Israel had prepared tactical nuclear warheads for use during an adverse phase of the 1973 Arab–Israeli conflict. Some of these reports came from normally reliable sources linked with US intelligence agencies, but it has been suggested that the event was an elaborate bluff by the Israeli authorities to encourage US support during the war.

An assessment of Israel's nuclear weapons potential was made in a report prepared under the aegis of the UN Secretary-General (*Study on Israeli Nuclear Armament*, United Nations, New York, 1982, A/36/431) which commented on Israel's known reactor programme. This includes the Nahel-Soreq research reactor. IRR–1, a light-water reactor provided by the United States and using 90 per cent enriched uranium. This reactor and its associated facilities are subject to safeguards agreed between the US, Israel and the International Atomic Energy Agency.

More significant is the IRR–2 reactor at Dimona, south-east of Beersheba in the Negev Desert. This is a natural uranium research reactor which is heavy-water moderated and had an initial thermal capacity of about 25 megawatts. The reactor was originally con-

structed in the early 1960s with the aid of French technical assistance and went into operation in December 1963.

While the UN report referred to above states that it is concerned with Israel's theoretical rather than actual nuclear weapons capability, it states that:

> Calculating on the basis of its original capacity (which may have been increased) the Dimona Reactor is capable of producing annually 8 to 10 kilograms of plutonium containing 70% of the fissile isotope 239. In the period from 1963 to present, around 100 kilograms could thus have been produced (assuming 6 to 8 months of operation a year). In light of the various possibilities of plutonium reprocessing listed . . . it is physically possible that Israel now possesses enough separated plutonium to manufacture 10 to 15 nuclear warheads.

Elsewhere, however, the report points out that there are reports that the reactor may have been increased to 70 megawatts giving an annual plutonium production equivalent to 3 nuclear weapons. The Dimona reactor is not subject to international safeguards.

Until late 1986, the general consensus would have been that Israel had had a capability to produce nuclear weapons since at least the early 1970s and had developed an arsenal of more than 30 weapons. Non-governmental sources within Israel gave much higher figures, of the order of 100 nuclear weapons.

In late 1986, information from a former technician at the Dimona plant was made public in Britain. This confirmed Dimona as the site of Israel's nuclear weapons production facility, providing details of a large underground facility. The Dimona reactor was assessed, according to this source, at well over 120 megawatts, and Israel's nuclear arsenal at between 100 and 200 warheads, including thermonuclear weapons.

A separate report quoted a former head of the French atomic energy programme as saying that the underground facility included a plutonium reprocessing facility built with French aid and similar to the French plant at Marcoule. Both reports may be regarded as broadly reliable.

Israel has a variety of means of delivering nuclear weapons, including missiles and strike aircraft, the most important examples being listed below. In addition to these, Israel has 131 *F–4E Phantoms*, 75 *F–16s* and 130 *A–4N/J Skyhawks*, all of which could be adapted to carry nuclear weapons. Furthermore, Israel's widely used Gabriel anti-ship missile and its extensive experience with

remotely-piloted vehicles provides it with the means to develop, if required, cruise missiles which could be used for nuclear warhead delivery.

Aircraft and Missiles

Kfir

The Kfir is an indigenous interceptor and close support aircraft developed in Israel in the late 1960s and early 1970s and based on the Mirage 5. It has a range of 1,500 miles in the ground attack configuration and is supersonic at low altitude. Almost certainly nuclear-capable, the Kfir remains in production, the latest version being the Kfir 7. Israel currently deploys 150 Kfirs in 5 squadrons with another 50 planes used for training. There are 60 more on order. The Kfir has 9 underwing and underfuselage hardpoints for bombs, missiles, rockets and other stores, and a typical load could include 2 1,000-lb bombs. Such a capability, given the necessary arming and control systems, would suffice for a kiloton-range nuclear weapon.

Lavie

The Lavie is the next generation of attack aircraft after the Kfir and is broadly similar to the US F–16. The Lavie will have a greater weapons load and combat radius than the Kfir and must be assumed to be nuclear-capable. The aircraft first flew early in 1987 but the development programme has run into considerable financial difficulties, with waning support in the US Congress. An original requirement of 260 has been reduced to 212 with deliveries due to commence in 1989. The Lavie will replace the A–4 Skyhawk and the Kfir.

F–15/F–16

While Israel may prefer to maintain its nuclear capability based on indigenous aircraft, its most capable aircraft are currently the F–15 and F–16. In USAF service both are nuclear-capable, and Israel could undertake the minor modifications to its own aircraft. Israel deploys 50 F–15s and 75 F–16s with a further 75 F–16s on order.

Jericho (MD–660)

The Jericho missile appears to have been developed, initially at least, with the French Dassault company during the 1960s and to have been operational by the end of that decade. It is broadly similar to the Lance missile (which is also in service in Israel) though less accurate. It has a substantially longer range than Lance, at 280 to 300 miles, and is reported to be a ramp-launched 2-stage solid-fuel missile deployed on a mobile launcher. It can carry a payload of 1,000 to 1,500 lb, reportedly adequate for a 20-kiloton nuclear warhead. A longer-range version, the Jericho MD–620, has been reported, development having commenced in the 1970s. It was tested over a 510 mile Mediterranean range in May 1987, but its full range is believed to be around 900 miles. Up to 100 Jericho II (MD 620) missiles may now be in service, though not all may be nuclear-armed. The range is sufficient to reach Baghdad.

Cruise Missiles

There have been occasional reports of a 1,200-mile-range cruise missile being developed by Israel for use as a nuclear delivery vehicle. None of these has been confirmed, but, in view of the strengths of Israel's indigenous armaments industry it would be unwise to discount them. Collaboration between Israel, South Africa and Taiwan has been suggested, but this is unlikely.

Artillery

Uncorroborated reports from non-governmental sources within Israel suggest an interest in nuclear-capable artillery, possibly in conjunction with South Africa. Israel's close military links with South African and the limited evidence of the low-kiloton 1979 nuclear detonation in the South Atlantic provide some support for this.

South Africa

Although there is no conclusive evidence, a number of factors support the view that South Africa has had a nuclear weapons capability since the early 1980s. The major development period was during the 1970s when there appears to have been close cooperation with Israel, and it is probable that South Africa has concentrated on free-fall nuclear weapons but with an interest in nuclear-capable artillery.

South Africa's commitment to nuclear weapons was at a time when the main threat to its security appeared to be from states to the north, especially after the collapse of the Portuguese regimes in Mozambique and Angola, and the achievement of black majority rule in Zimbabwe. In the 1980s, South Africa has perceived the major threat to its security as being more internal. A result of this may have been a decreased financial commitment to the development of a large nuclear weapons arsenal and, for example, the development of fusion weapons.

In summary, South Africa probably has a small number of nuclear weapons, certainly fewer than 50, or could assemble them rapidly if required. It has appropriate delivery systems.

Evidence for a South African nuclear weapons programme accumulated in the late 1970s. On 3 and 4 July 1977, a Soviet Cosmos 922 satellite was used to scan the Kalahari Desert and on 2 August of that year a Cosmos 932 was used on a similar mission. As a result of these surveys, the Soviet Union reported that South Africa was close to conducting a nuclear weapons test. The United States subsequently used similar reconnaissance methods and produced corroborating evidence.

There is evidence to suggest that South Africa was then subjected to strong diplomatic pressure from the Carter administration in the United States, together with the governments of Britain, France and West Germany as well as the Soviet Union. As a result of this pressure, no test was recorded as taking place, but South Africa did

not allow international inspection of the 'test site'.

Two years later, on 22 September 1979, a US VELA high-altitude satellite recorded radiation emissions consistent with a low-yield (2 to 4 kilotons) nuclear detonation in the South Atlantic. The satellite concerned is one of two placed in orbit some nine years previously in order to monitor compliance with the 1963 Partial Test Ban Treaty. Following this 1979 event, the US Department of State issued the following statement on 25 October of that year:

> The United States Government has an indication suggesting the possibility that a low yield nuclear explosion occurred on September 22 in the area of the Indian Ocean and the South Atlantic including portions of the Antarctic continent and the southern part of Africa. No corroborating evidence has been received to date. We are continuing to assess whether such an event took place.

A subsequent examination of the available data by a US Presidential Review Group concluded that the event recorded was probably not a nuclear explosion, but, according to a UN report published a year later, the matter remained an open question. The UN report drew attention to evidence that a South African naval task-force was operating in the area at the time of the presumed test, and it has been suggested that the event was actually a test of a small nuclear warhead, detonated at low altitude, possibly conducted in association with Israel. Other sources suggest that it was connected with the development of an artillery shell, but the small size of the detonation could simply result from a restricted-yield test of a larger device.

At a more general level, South Africa is theoretically capable of following either the plutonium or uranium routes to nuclear weapons. Regarding the former, South Africa has a research reactor, the SAFARI–1, at Pelindaba, constructed with US help, which went critical in 1965 but has been covered by IAEA safeguards since 1967. There is also an indigenously designed Palindaba-Zero reactor which went critical in 1967 and was in operation for a few years.

A large nuclear power-plant has been built by a French consortium at Koeberg, north-west of Cape Town, which has twin pressurised water reactors rated at 922 megawatts. This plant is covered by a tri-partite safeguards agreement between France, South Africa and the IAEA which came into force in 1977. It follows that there are limitations on South Africa's using the plutonium route to nuclear weapons, but it would be unwise to suggest that these

limitations are total.

Concerning the uranium route, South Africa, together with Namibia which it still controls, is one of the world's major suppliers of uranium from its own mines, and it also has a long history of work on uranium enrichment. A pilot enrichment plant was established at Valindaba in the early 1970s under the aegis of the Uranium Enrichment Corporation of South Africa (UCOR), the process being described as a modification of the West German Becker nozzle process.

While there is no unequivocal evidence that the Valindaba plant has been used to produce enriched uranium for weapons production, a UN report in 1980, *South Africa's Plans and Capability in the Nuclear Field* (UN, New York, A/35/402) estimated that the plant, which commenced operations in April 1975 and reached full capacity two years later, could have produced sufficient material for at least 1 bomb by August 1977 and perhaps 8 bombs by the end of 1980.

A much larger semi-commercial plant at Valindaba was due to commence operations during 1987. The South African authorities state that the plant is designed purely to enrich natural uranium to an extent necessary for nuclear power-plant fuel rather than the much more highly enriched weapons grade.

The aim would be to make the Koeberg nuclear power-plant independent of foreign supplies of enriched uranium. This is plausible but a SIPRI report in November 1986 suggested that two other purposes might be production of enriched uranium for export or as a bargaining counter with Western countries. The plant could also be used to produce weapons grade uranium and the SIPRI source suggested that a laser enrichment process was also being investigated at Valindaba.

Finally, there are occasional reports that South Africa is interested in enhanced radiation warheads, possibly in the context of artillery shells, and in collaboration with Israel. These remain unconfirmed.

Delivery Systems

While South Africa's possession of nuclear weapons has not been confirmed, it is likely. Regarding delivery systems, there are appropriate means of delivering free-fall nuclear weapons and artillery shells.

South Africa operates 5 *Canberra* and 6 *Buccaneer* bombers and 32 *Mirage F–1AZ* in the fighter/ground attack role. The navy's 12 fast attack craft carry a version of the Israeli Gabriel missile but it is unlikely that South Africa could, unaided, produce missile-based nuclear delivery systems.

South Africa maintains an interest in highly mobile self-propelled artillery, the main example being the *G–6* 155 mm howitzer, developed originally by the US-based Space Research Corporation. The G–6 carries a crew of 5, has a 6-wheeled chassis, a top speed of over 60 m.p.h. and considerable cross-country ability. If South Africa was to develop AFAPs for the G–6, they would make a formidable and potentially devastating combination. The G–6 entered service with the South African Army in 1983 and at least 10 are now in service.

India

India became the world's sixth acknowledged nuclear power on 17 May 1974 with the successful test-firing of a nuclear device rated at under 15 kilotons in an underground test conducted in the Rajasthan Desert. Since then, the Indian government has persistently denied that India has utilised its obvious expertise in producing a nuclear weapons arsenal. Many analysts doubt this, but it must also be admitted that the Indian government has maintained a markedly anti-nuclear posture in its foreign relations, including participation in the Four Continents Peace Initiative.

The current context, however, is of a China which is expanding its nuclear forces, including the deployment of SSBN. A more immediate concern is the Pakistani nuclear weapons programme and it is probably true that a demonstrated nuclear weapons ability by Pakistan would be sufficient for India to announce the existence of a small nuclear arsenal. Until now, however, it may well be that India has developed the ability to produce nuclear weapons but does not maintain a stock of assembled weapons.

India has a substantial indigenous defence industry and maintains a large and expanding space programme, the latter providing it with the technology to produce intermediate-range ballistic missiles. While it maintains a close relationship with the Soviet Union in relation to defence procurement and space activities, it has, during the 1980s, involved itself more strongly with the UK and France.

Aircraft

India has a substantial number of planes which could be adapted for a nuclear attack role. Many of India's new strike aircraft are produced under licence from the Soviet Union, Britain and France. The air force has 3 bomber and 11 FGA squadrons and the planes

include 35 *Canberra*, 68 *Jaguar* and 72 *MiG–23 BN Flogger H*. 40 *Mirage 2000H* are being deployed and India introduced the *MiG–27M* into service early in 1986. Around 200 of these planes will eventually be deployed. Plans for an indigenous *Light Combat Aircraft* (LCA) continue but the first flight will not now be until the early 1990s. While the plane is optimised for interception, it will have a secondary ground attack role. It is unlikely to be nuclear-capable but indicates the technical capabilities of the Indian defence industry.

The Indian Navy operates 1 aircraft-carrier, *Vikrant*, which can carry 8 Sea Harriers. These aircraft are in service with the British Navy in a nuclear-capable configuration. India has acquired *Hermes* from the UK as its second carrier, renamed *Viraat*, and has 10 more Sea Harriers on order.

Space Activities

India has an active space programme, although its aims have been subject to delays. Indigenous satellites were initially launched using Soviet launchers, but work on a small satellite launch vehicle commenced as early as 1973. This evolved into the SLV–3, a 4-stage solid-fuel rocket capable of putting an 85-lb payload into low orbit, which was used successfully from 1980 onwards.

A development of the SLV–3 is the Augmented Satellite Launch Vehicle (ASLV) which is essentially an SLV–3 with the addition of 2 strap-on solid-fuel boosters derived from the SLV first stage. It is designed to launch a 320-lb satellite but the first launch failed in March 1987, and a second attempt was scheduled for 1988. A further development will be the Polar Satellite Launch Vehicle (PSLV) which will be able to place a 2,200-lb satellite into a 650-mile-altitude polar sun-synchronous orbit. The substantial PSLV will weigh 275 tons at launch and should be launched for the first time in 1990. India hopes to complete a launcher capable of putting a 5,500-lb satellite into geo-synchronous orbit by the early 1990s.

Missile Development

The description of India's space activities is intended to indicate

India's ability to produce ballistic missiles. It has been reported that the Defence Research and Development Laboratory at Hyderabad is working on a defence-related rocket. The programme includes the static test of a powerful liquid-fuel twin-chamber rocket-motor and the construction, at a cost of $250 million, of a missile range at Chorbalia in Orissa including a tracking station in the Nilgiri Hills.

Pakistan

Throughout the period from 1984 to 1986 there were persistent reports, especially in the US press, that Pakistan was developing nuclear weapons, and many of these reports linked Pakistan's research and development programme to technical assistance from China. The Pakistan government routinely denied these reports, but a leaked Defence Intelligence Agency document, contents of which were published in Washington, supported the earlier reports in two ways.

According to this, the Kahuta nuclear research complex near Islamabad had developed the capability to produce 93.5 per cent enriched uranium, a weapons grade enrichment. Furthermore, Pakistan had developed and tested the conventional explosive arrays necessary to produce the implosion effect triggering a fission reaction. The Pakistan government denied this report. In particular, it insisted that the Kahuta plant was only concerned with producing the very much lower level of uranium enrichment — 3.0 to 3.5 per cent — necessary for the Cheshma nuclear power facility.

In March 1987, President Zia ul-Haq, denied that Pakistan had a nuclear weapons programme while acknowledging that Pakistan had the technical ability to produce nuclear weapons.

In spite of official denials, a consensus of opinion among analysts of nuclear proliferation would be that Pakistan has had a nuclear weapons programme since the mid-1970s and has had, possibly from 1986, the ability to produce a nuclear weapons device. It is possible that a small arsenal of nuclear weapons is now being produced.

Delivery Systems

The Pakistan Air Force has a range of aircraft types which could be adapted as nuclear-capable delivery vehicles. They include 17 *Mirage III*, 50 *Mirage 5* and 41 of the Chinese *Nanchang Q–5*. Pakistan

also has 170 *Shenyang J–6*, although their primary function is the interceptor role. The most capable plane in the inventory is the US *F–16*. Two squadrons are in service with 40 aircraft, and Pakistan is seeking a further 40. The F–16 is also primarily an interceptor, but the USAF has it in a nuclear-capable configuration, and Pakistan could undertake the minor adaptions to its own planes. The F–16 would be the plane most capable of penetrating Indian air defences in the event of a conflict.

Argentina and Brazil

Argentina and Brazil have long been regarded as rivals in a race to become the first Latin American state to develop nuclear weapons, but there is evidence that the recent easing of relations between the countries may have lead to a curbing of their nuclear weapons programmes.

In terms of nuclear technology, Argentina is probably the more advanced. In addition to domestic nuclear power reactors, it has a small-scale uranium enrichment programme which certainly reached a 1 per cent enrichment level by 1983. In March 1987 it was reported that Argentina could be a source of 20 per cent enriched uranium to be offered to Iran, under IAEA safeguards, for use in the charging of a small research reactor in Tehran. In addition, the state-owned nuclear reactor construction company, Enace, is part of an international consortium bidding to complete Iran's 1,000 megawatt Bushehr 1 nuclear power-plant.

Argentina's weapons programme appears to have made considerable progress under the various military juntas in power until 1983. Since then, there is strong evidence that the civilian government of President Alfonsin has slowed down the programme. Moreover, the summit meeting between Alfonsin and President Sarney of Brazil in July 1986 appears to have lead to an informal understanding by both leaders to delay the completion of nuclear weapons programmes.

In the early 1980s Brazil was believed to be three to four years behind Argentina in its programme, but in 1986 it was reported that it was preparing a test site for an underground nuclear detonation. Brazil is also in the early stages of developing an indigenous nuclear-powered submarine. This is likely to go ahead but, at the time of writing, there is some optimism that a regional nuclear arms race between Brazil and Argentina may have been curbed.

If nuclear weapons were to be developed by either country, appropriate delivery systems would be easy to adapt from their air

force inventories. Interestingly, both countries have active rocket programmes, currently directed towards space research. Argentina has been reported to have a rocket which could be developed into a 500-mile-range system, and Brazil's Sondoco series, particularly the Sondoco IV, could even be developed into a limited-range ICBM.

Overseas Basing and Proliferation

While proliferation is normally taken to mean the spread of nuclear weapons by means of countries acquiring the technical ability to produce their own nuclear weapons, there are two other forms of proliferation to be considered. One is the practice of overseas basing of weapons and delivery systems. The other is the practice of overseas basing of weapons intended for use with delivery systems held by a close ally. The United States, the Soviet Union and the United Kingdom engage in the former, and the United States and the Soviet Union allow the latter.

Maritime basing of nuclear weapons is a common practice by the United States, the Soviet Union, the United Kingdom and France and has recently been practised by China with its deployment of an indigenous SSBN capability. All 5 countries have SSBN, and deployment areas include the Atlantic, Pacific and Arctic Oceans and the Mediterranean Sea. The United States and China may deploy SSBN to the Indian Ocean. Major surface vessels of the United States, the Soviet Union, the United Kingdom and France carry tactical nuclear weapons and the first 2 countries have nuclear-armed attack submarines. Ordnance includes torpedoes, gravity bombs, surface-to-air missiles, anti-ship missiles, land attack missiles and depth-bombs. Ships armed with tactical nuclear weapons are deployed throughout the world, but principally in the northern hemisphere.

The United States makes most use of overseas land-based deployment of nuclear weapons, especially in Western Europe, although the Soviet Union has increased its overseas nuclear basing commitments during the mid-1980s.

Soviet Union/Warsaw Pact

The Soviet Union has extensive tactical nuclear forces deployed for

use against NATO. The practice used to be for the delivery systems to be forward-based but the nuclear warheads retained in the Soviet Union. This appears still to be the case with most systems, especially artillery, but nuclear weapons stores are now considered to be located in a number of Eastern European countries.

Angola

Regular naval and occasional air force deployments. No nuclear weapons stored but nuclear-armed ships use port facilities.

Bulgaria

The Bulgarian Army has 40 FROG–7 and 36 Scud missile launchers which may be nuclear-capable, but nuclear warheads do not appear to be located at any sites in Bulgaria.

Cuba

Nuclear weapons are not deployed in Cuba although nuclear-capable aircraft such as the Bear–F ASW plane do deploy to 2 airfields and nuclear-armed ships visit Cuban ports.

Czechoslovakia

The Czechoslovak Army has 27 Scud missile launchers and 40 FROG launchers, the latter converting to SS–21, and the Czech Air Force has 3 squadrons with 50 Su–7 nuclear-capable aircraft. Soviet forces maintain SS–12M and Scud/SS–23 missiles and 45 MiG–27 nuclear-capable aircraft, all with nuclear weapons deployed in Czechoslovakia.

East Germany

The GDR armed forces have 24 Scud and 24 FROG–7 launchers, the latter converting to SS–21, and the Group of Soviet Forces in Germany (GSFG) maintain both SS–12M and SS–23 launchers. GSFG maintain large numbers of nuclear-capable aircraft in the GDR, including several hundred Su–17, Su–24 and MiG–27. At least 7 air-bases are believed to have nuclear weapons storage facilities.

Ethiopia/South Yemen

Nuclear-armed ships probably use Dahlak Island naval facility, a support base for Soviet naval operations in the Indian Ocean, and also port facilities in Aden. Il–38 May ASW planes operate from bases in both countries. It is unlikely that nuclear store facilities exist in either country.

Hungary

The Hungarian Army deploys 24 FROG–7 and 9 Scud launchers. Soviet forces operate FROG–7, SS–21 and Scud missiles and 90 Su–17 and Su–24 nuclear-capable aircraft. Nuclear artillery units also operate in Hungary but it is not clear whether there are any permanent nuclear weapons storage sites in Hungary.

Mongolia

Soviet ground forces deploy FROG–7 launchers in Mongolia but there are no indications of nuclear weapons storage sites.

Poland

The Polish Army has 56 FROG and 32 Scud B launchers and the Air Force has 40 Su–7 aircraft. Soviet forces in Poland include a battalion equipped with Scud missile launchers. There are conflicting reports about the deployment of nuclear-capable aircraft with the Soviet Air Force in Poland, but one report suggests deployment of Su–24 nuclear-capable aircraft and nuclear weapons storage sites at 2 air-bases.

Romania

The Romanian Army has 30 FROG and 15 Scud launchers. There are no Soviet forces based in Romania and it is unlikely that nuclear weapons would be released to the Romanian armed forces.

Vietnam

The Cam Ranh Bay naval base and airfield and the Da Nang air-base all support nuclear-capable systems. Naval deployments

average 20 to 25 vessels, but most of these are minor surface combatants and auxiliaries. Fewer than 10 nuclear-capable submarines and surface ships operate out of the base. Air force deployments include 8 Tu–95 Bear and 16 Tu–16 Badger aircraft, principally in an MR/ASW role.

United States/NATO

The United States has a much higher level of deployment of nuclear weapons overseas, especially in Europe. Unlike the Soviet Union, many of its ships and submarines operate continually from overseas bases and many of these have nuclear weapons stores attached to them. Excluding the fleet ballistic missile submarines at Holy Loch in Scotland, US nuclear weapons deployed in Europe in early 1987 are detailed in Table 7 (below), these figures assuming that the withdrawal of obsolete weapons agreed at the 1983 Monte Bello NATO meeting had been completed.

Table 7 US nuclear weapons in Europe

Weapons	Warhead numbers		
	US use	Allied use	Total
Bombs	1,416	324	1,740
Depth-bombs	129	63	192
Pershing 2	108	0	108
GLCM	208	0	208
Pershing 1A	0	100	100
Lance	324	368	692
203 mm AFAP	506	432	938
155 mm AFAP	594	138	732
Enhanced radiation warheads *	c.600		c.600
Total	3,885	1,425	5,310

* ER warheads for Lance missile and 203 mm howitzers stored at Seneca Arsenal, New York State specifically for deployment in the European theatre.

The following gives an indication, probably incomplete, of overseas basing of nuclear weapons by the United States.

Belgium

The Belgian Army has 168 M109 and 11 M110 howitzers and the Air Force has 72 F–16 aircraft. Kleine Brogel air-base has a US nuclear weapons store for the Belgian F–16s. Florennes is the base for Belgian cruise missiles; the full complement will be 48 missiles on 12 launchers.

Canada

Canada formerly had Genie nuclear-tipped air-to-air missiles, maintained in US custody, for its CF–101 Voodoo interceptors. Their replacements, the CF–18 Hornets, are not nuclear-armed and Canada has thus given up its nuclear role. US cruise missiles are tested in flight over Canadian territory.

Bermuda

Kindley Naval Air Station receives regular deployments of P–3 Orion ASW aircraft. Unconfirmed reports indicate that there would be a nuclear weapons store in Bermuda in time of war.

Diego Garcia

The development of Diego Garcia into a major base for US Central Command (covering South West Asia and North East Africa) involves logistic support for a carrier battle group and a marine amphibious brigade, both deploying tactical nuclear weapons. Diego Garcia is also reported to be designated as a nuclear weapons storage site for depth-bombs for P3 Orion ASW aircraft in time of war.

Greece

There are no US nuclear warheads for use with US forces in Greece, but US warheads are maintained for Greek forces. The Greek Army has 108 M109, 32 M110 and 40 M115 howitzers and the Air Force has 66 F–104 nuclear-capable aircraft. Nuclear-tipped Honest John and Nike-Hercules missiles are being withdrawn as obsolete. The Nike-Hercules missiles are being replaced with conventionally-armed surface-to-air missiles. The Honest John artillery missiles may be replaced by Lance missiles, but this has not been confirmed.

Guam

Guam is the main nuclear weapons base for the western Pacific. Andersen air-base is the only base outside the United States deploying B–52 bombers. These are equipped with gravity bombs and SRAMs. Apra Harbour is a major naval base and includes a nuclear-capable stores ship. Santa Rita is a naval magazine which stores bombs and depth-bombs for navy use and AFAPs for the marines.

Italy

Comiso in Sicily will be the base for 112 cruise missiles; 96 had been deployed there by early 1987. The port of Gaeta is the main base for the US Sixth Fleet which operates many nuclear-armed surface ships. La Maddalena on Sardinia is a base for US attack submarines and is a nuclear weapons store for SUBROC missiles. A major nuclear weapons store at Aviano air-base supports nuclear-capable F–16s rotated from Spain. A wide range of nuclear warheads is in US custody in Italy for potential use with a variety of systems deployed by the Italian armed forces. These include 6 Lance missile launchers with perhaps 42 missiles and over 250 nuclear-capable howitzers. There are 54 Tornado and 18 F–104 strike aircraft in service in the FGA role and they can carry free-fall nuclear bombs. Nuclear depth-bombs are deployed in Italy for use with 14 Atlantic ASW aircraft as well as Nimrod and P–3 Orion ASW aircraft which can be deployed to Italy from the UK and USA respectively. Around 500 nuclear warheads of all types are believed to be deployed in Italy by the United States.

Japan

There are no US nuclear weapons permanently stored in Japan, but nuclear-armed major surface vessels regularly use Japanese ports and Marine Corps artillery and a variety of nuclear-capable planes are based in Japan. There is reported to be a contingency nuclear weapons store for nuclear depth-bombs at Misawa air-base.

Netherlands

The Dutch Army has 218 M–109 and 76 M–110 howitzers which

can fire AFAPs, and also has 6 Lance missile launchers with 42 missiles. The air force has 119 F–16 nuclear-capable strike aircraft with a further 81 on order. The naval air arm has 13 P–3 Orion aircraft which can deliver nuclear depth-bombs but it is reported that the nuclear role for these planes has been relinquished. There are to be 48 GLCMs based at Woensdrecht air-base from 1988.

Philippines

Clark air-base and Subic Bay naval base form 2 of the largest overseas military bases of the US armed forces. Nuclear-capable ships and planes are deployed in the Philippines but nuclear weapons are not currently stored there. Contingency storage facilities exist at Clark, Subic Bay and the naval air station at Cubi Point.

South Korea

Nuclear-capable army and air force units are based in South Korea, including 155 mm and 208 mm artillery and F–16 strike aircraft. Nuclear weapons for these systems are stored at Kunsan air-base which is reported to house around 150 warheads.

Turkey

Because of its location close to the Soviet Union, Turkey is a major forward operating base for nuclear-armed strike aircraft of the US Air Force. Around 400 nuclear warheads, mainly bombs, are stored in Turkey, about half of them at Incirlik air-base. Some of the nuclear warheads are for use by Turkish armed forces which are equipped with over 200 howitzers. The air force has 90 F–4s and 40 F–100s in the FGA role.

United Kingdom

The USAF operates 84 F–111s from Lakenheath and 72 from Upper Heyford; each base stores around 300 nuclear warheads.

The Bentwaters/Woodbridge base is reported to be assigned a nuclear warhead storage facility in the future. Around 60 nuclear depth-bombs are stored at each of 2 sites, Machrihanish and St Mawgan, for use by US P–3 Orion and RAF Nimrod ASW aircraft. Poseidon missile submarines operate from Holy Loch. There are

normally 3 boats with 510 warheads in the loch at any one time, but it is estimated that 7 boats are deployed from the missile submarine tender based there, these boats having 1,120 warheads. Holy Loch is now the only US SSBN base outside the United States. There are 96 GLCMs operational at Greenham Common with 64 scheduled for Molesworth.

West Germany

There are more nuclear warheads located in West Germany than in any other non-nuclear country, with around 3,000 stored there in 1987. Most are US warheads intended for use by US forces and by allied forces based in West Germany. The United States operates nuclear-capable artillery, Lance missiles and aircraft in West Germany, and it will be an important base for the F–15E Strike Eagle, probably the world's most advanced nuclear-capable strike aircraft. The USAF operates 108 Pershing 2 missile launchers, and 96 GLCMs will be operational at Wüschheim, deployment having commenced with a 16-missile flight in 1986. The West German armed forces have 100 Pershing 1A missiles with 72 launchers, over 800 M–109 and M–110 howitzers, 26 Lance missile launchers with perhaps 150 missiles, 90 F–104 and over 100 Tornado FGA aircraft.

United Kingdom

In time of war, UK ASW aircraft could be forward based in *Bermuda*, *Cyprus*, *Gibraltar*, and *Iceland*. Gibraltar has been reported to house a temporary nuclear weapons storage facility but this is unconfirmed. Cyprus used to be a major base for nuclear-armed V-bombers and storage facilities may still exist although not currently in use. Nuclear-capable Buccaneer strike aircraft do deploy to Cyprus.

In West Germany, the BAOR is reported to have 101 M–109 and 16 M–110 howitzers and 12 Lance missile launchers with perhaps 84 missiles, all these being capable of firing US nuclear warheads. Eight Tornado squadrons are being based in West Germany, all but one in the strike role, and these can carry the British WE177 free-fall nuclear bomb, storage facilities being reported at RAF Bruggen. RAF Gutersloh will receive over 60 Harrier GR5 aircraft during the late 1980s. Unlike the earlier Harriers these are nuclear-capable,

although the UK Ministry of Defence has stated that they do not currently plan to deploy them with a nuclear role.

Proliferation

This guide has documented the nuclear arsenals of the 2 major nuclear powers, the United States and the Soviet Union, the 3 middle-ranking nuclear powers, Britain, France and China, and 3 countries which have or could rapidly assemble nuclear weapons, Israel, South Africa and India. It has also commented on 3 near-nuclear powers, Pakistan, Argentina and Brazil. Although the guide is concerned with existing nuclear powers it is appropriate to discuss briefly the possible tendencies towards future proliferation. In doing so, it is appropriate to recognise two classes of country.

One is that group which has, or could readily acquire, the technology to produce nuclear weapons, but does not pursue that path. There are many such countries, some in nuclear alliances, others neutral. Many of the former have nuclear weapons based on the territory and possibly available under a dual control system to their own military forces. They include Italy, Greece the Netherlands and West Germany. Some countries which are closely allied to nuclear powers do not allow foreign nuclear weapons on their territory yet do not seek to become nuclear powers themselves. They include Australia, Japan, Canada and Spain. New Zealand takes an even stronger line and will not allow nuclear-armed ships into its territorial waters.

Perhaps the most interesting are those countries which are broadly in the Western economic system, are politically neutral but are close to Warsaw Pact territory. These countries, such as Sweden and Switzerland, which could be considered at risk from the Soviet bloc, have the technical proficiency to develop nuclear weapons, but have chosen, so far, not to do so. Indeed they tend to be markedly opposed to nuclear weapons. In summary, then, there are many countries which *could* have developed nuclear weapons but have decided not to do so.

The second group of states appears to be interested in developing nuclear weapons but has not yet succeeded in doing so. It is from the ranks of these countries that future nuclear weapons states will be drawn and it is appropriate to consider, briefly, the more significant contenders.

Iran

Under the Shah, Iran developed a major nuclear industry and was certainly in the early stages of developing nuclear weapons. The revolution and the Iran–Iraq war combined to curb, if not completely curtail, this programme but it appears that minor elements of it remained intact and, given more stable circumstances, Iran will once again engage in a nuclear weapons programme. Two partially-completed nuclear power-plants at Bushehr were halted in 1979 but work has continued at the Tehran Research Centre which includes a small research reactor, likely to be supplied with enriched uranium by Argentina. A second nuclear research centre opened in 1984 at Isfahan and it is clear that even the problems caused by the Gulf War have not halted Iran's research programme, merely delayed it.

Iraq

Iraq embarked on a major expansion of its nuclear programme in the mid-1970s, concentrating apparently on developing a nuclear power programme. In reality, its objective appears to have been much more concerned with developing nuclear weapons, and the Osiraq research reactor near Baghdad was integral to this. This reactor was destroyed in an Israeli air raid in February 1981 and has not been rebuilt. This, combined with the very heavy commitments to the Gulf War have meant that Iraq's nuclear weapons plans have been severely hindered. Should the war end without Iraq's defeat, the programme could be started up again with results within perhaps five years.

Libya

Libya has made efforts to acquire nuclear weapons technology and these have extended to agreements with Pakistan involving Libyan financing of Pakistan's nuclear programme with the supply of nuclear technology in return. Libya has also attempted to acquire appropriate technology on the international market. All the evidence suggests that the results have been extremely limited, even in relation to Pakistan, and that Libya has no near-term prospects of developing nuclear weapons. The intention to do so remains.

Egypt

There is little direct evidence of an Egyptian commitment to developing nuclear weapons, although some observers suggest that regional geopolitics would encourage such a commitment. Egypt and Brazil completed a nuclear cooperation accord in 1986, apparently involving just civil nuclear technology. More importantly, a research agreement has been concluded between Egypt, Iraq and Pakistan which will involve the building of an experimental reactor at Al-Wadi Al-Jadid in Egypt. This again is said to be for civil purposes only, but it does link Egypt with two states having known nuclear weapons ambitions.

Taiwan

Taiwan remains something approaching a garrison state and has the highest defence spending in Asia as a percentage of GDP. In the period 1966–75 Taiwan was intent on developing nuclear technology with a view to producing nuclear weapons. Many attempts to buy in such technology were countered by direct or indirect pressure from the United States. During the early 1980s, the Taiwan government maintained that it did not have a nuclear weapons programme although in 1983 the President told foreign correspondents that his country did have the technological capability to do so.

South Korea and North Korea

South Korea's relationship with the United States is closer than is that of Taiwan. This enables the United States to exert greater control over any possible South Korean nuclear ambitions. A nuclear weapons programme does appear to have existed in its early stages in the early 1970s, but US pressure appears to have curtailed this, and South Korea finally ratified the Non-Proliferation Treaty in 1976.

In the early 1980s, concern grew that North Korea's large Yong Byon research reactor, an obsolete design but one useful in a nuclear weapons programme, signified a North Korean intent to develop nuclear weapons. It appears that United States diplomats attempted to persuade the Soviet Union to exert pressure on North Korea to ratify the NPT. North Korea did so in December 1985. This may help to dissuade South Korea from renewing its interest in

a nuclear weapons programme but, given the technological capability of South Korea, any future decision to develop nuclear weapons could result in rapid progress.

Postscript

Arms Control

Progress towards an INF treaty in late 1987 suggested that upwards of 2,000 missile warheads might be withdrawn by the early 1990s. While this represents barely 4 per cent of world nuclear arsenals, and is a figure which will be exceeded easily by other weapons programmes, it is significant for two reasons. One is that it will be the first time that modern as distinct from obsolete nuclear weapons will have been withdrawn as the result of a treaty. The second is that a wide range of important verification procedures will be implemented which can be applied to other classes of nuclear weapons.

Even so, plans are under consideration to compensate for the withdrawal of weapons by deploying other weapons not covered by the treaty. Options discussed at the NATO Nuclear Planning Group meeting at Monterey, California, in November 1987 are believed to have included submarine-launched cruise missiles, air-launched cruise missiles and nuclear-capable strike aircraft, all to be deployed from bases in Europe. The British Trident missile force would be a suitable targeting replacement for the Pershing 2 missiles, but this and the other compensation measures may meet with forceful public opposition in Europe.

The best prospect is that the INF treaty will be followed rapidly by deep cuts in strategic arsenals *and* by rapid progress towards a comprehensive test ban and a freezing of new deployments. Unfortunately the evidence presented in this volume suggests a substantial momentum in the nuclear arms race which may prove difficult to reverse.

Armaments

United States

M–X Peacekeeper ICBMs are expected to be fitted with earth-penetrating warheads by the mid-1990s. It has been confirmed that the USAF is bringing the 9-megaton *B53* bomb back into service for use against hardened targets, especially deep underground command bunkers. If Trident SLBMs are included in future strategic arms control negotiations, *Ohio*-class submarines could be retrofitted with *sea-launched cruise missiles*, each Trident missile launch tube taking up to 7 SLCMs, giving 168 missiles per submarine. A USAF–DARPA project is researching a *Boost Glide* weapon involving an ICBM-launched upper atmosphere Mach 15 glide vehicle capable of low-altitude manoeuvrable targeting. The *Advanced Cruise Missile* (ACM) is reported to have a range of 2,300 miles. The *SRAM II* missile programme has experienced considerable problems and cancellation is possible.

Soviet Union

A test of the *SS–X–26* heavy ICBM was conducted in September 1987 but fell 1,000 miles short of the designated target area. A second *Sierra-class submarine* is reported to have been launched and to be engaged in trials. The *SS–N–22* anti-ship missile is being fitted to the *Tarantul–III* corvette. Previous *Tarantul* corvettes carried the *SS–N–2C*.

France

The *M–5* SLBM will carry 12 *TN 75* warheads. These will also equip the SSBS *S–4* missile from 1996.

United Kingdom

Unconfirmed reports suggest that the *M110 howitzer* will no longer be deployed in a nuclear-certified role. A reliable source indicates that the *Polaris/Chevaline* system has 2 warheads. It is also reported that estimates for the total UK nuclear arsenal of 200 warheads are too low, the actual figure being closer to earlier estimates of around 500.

Israel

The *Lavie* project has been cancelled but funds have been voted to maintain parts of the project and it may yet survive.

Strategic Nuclear Arsenals

Assessing the size of strategic nuclear arsenals is fraught with variables, and any attempt will result in no more than an approximation. Table 9 opposite gives an estimate for US and Soviet strategic nuclear warheads for January 1988, with figures for early 1984 given in brackets.

Table 8 below illustrates the variations between assessments, comparing figures from the present publication with those published late in 1987 by the International Institute for Strategic Studies and the US Arms Control Association. The variation is due largely to different yardsticks employed in assessing operational loadings of delivery systems, particularly long-range bombers.

Table 8 Strategic nuclear arsenals — three assessments

Source	ICBM	SLBM	Bombers	Total
United States				
IIS				
Nov. 87	2,261	6,656	4,956	13,873
ACA				
Oct. 87	2,268	5,632	3,886	11,786
Bradford				
Jan. 88	2,310	6,144	4,278	12,732
Soviet Union				
IIS				
Nov. 87	6,440	3,344	1,260	11,044
ACA				
Oct. 87	6,388	3,668	840	10,896
Bradford				
Jan. 88	6,470	3,272	670	10,412

All three assessments show the United States to have a lead over the Soviet Union in warhead numbers. Table 9 also shows that, between 1984 and 1988, the total arsenals increased by around 4,400, or about 24 per cent. This was at a time when the two countries were ostensibly negotiating on strategic arms control. Perhaps the next four years will be more fruitful.

Table 9 Strategic nuclear arsenals — estimate for January 1988

Delivery mode	Delivery system	Number of systems	Warheads per system	Total	
United States					
ICBM	Minuteman II	450	1	450	
	Minuteman III	520	3	1,560	
	M–X Peacekeeper	30	10	300	
				2,310	(2,136)[5]
SLBM	Poseidon C3	256	12[1]	3,072	
	Trident C4	384	8	3,072	
				6,144	(5,344)
Long-range aircraft	B52 G/H (non-ALCM)	113	14[2]	1,582	
	B52 G/H (ALCM)	150	12[3]	1,800	
	B1B	64	14[4]	896	
				4,278	(3,146)
		Total warheads		12,732	(10,626)
Soviet Union					
ICBM	SS–11	400	1	400	
	SS–13	60	1	60	
	SS–17	140[6]	4	560	
	SS–18	308	10	3,080	
	SS–19	360	6	2,160	
	SS–24	10	10	100	
	SS–25	110	1	110	
				6,479	(5,588)
SLBM	SS–N–6	256	1[7]	256	
	SS–N–8	292	1	292	
	SS–N–18	224	6[8]	1,344	
	SS–N–20	100	9[9]	900	
	SS–N–23	48	10	480	
				3,272	(2,309)
Long-range aircraft	Bear (non-ALCM)	100	3	300	
	Bear (ALCM)	55	6[10]	330	
	Bison	20	2	40	
				670	(209)
		Total warheads		10,412	(8,087)

Notes:

1. Poseidon C3 has 10–14 warheads. This assumes an average of 12.
2. The B–52 can take 24 nuclear weapons per sortie, but operational loadings are lower.
3. Can comprise gravity bombs as well as ALCMs.
4. Assumed operational loading. Maximum capacity is 38 nuclear weapons.
5. Figures in brackets are totals for early 1984.
6. Assumes 10 SS–17 missiles withdrawn to compensate for 10 SS–24 missiles deployed.
7. MRV warheads count as one per missile.
8. SS–N–18 is fitted with 3 or 7 warheads. This assumes most are 7-MIRV, giving an average of 6.
9. Assumes all missiles are fitted with the larger 9-MIRV system.
10. Maximum loading may be 8. Operational loading likely to be 4 or 6. This assumes the latter.

Sources

There were three main sources of information for this guide:

1. Books and Yearbooks

The annual surveys of the Stockholm International Peace Research Institute and the International Institute of Strategic Studies were generally useful. Similarly, the various 'Jane's' Yearbooks, especially *Fighting Ships*, *Weapons Systems* and *All the World's Aircraft*, contain a wealth of material. Some specialised books were of value, especially the *Nuclear Weapons Databook*, Volume 1, *US Nuclear Forces and Capabilities*, by T. B. Cochran, W. M. Arkin and M. M. Hoenig (Ballinger, Cambridge, Mass., 1987), which is a comprehensive study of current US nuclear forces. *Nuclear Battlefields*, by William Arkin and Richard Fieldhouse (Ballinger, Cambridge, Mass., 1985), gives a thorough listing of nuclear bases world-wide and, in the context of NATO deployments, Daniel Charles's recent volume, *Nuclear Planning in NATO* (Ballinger, Cambridge, Mass., 1987), is informative. Finally, Leonard Spector's *Going Nuclear* (Ballinger, Cambridge, MA, 1987) is the best single source on nuclear proliferation.

2. Journals

A wide range of technical and general journals was scanned. These included *Flight*, *Aviation Week*, *Interavia*, *International Defence Review*, *Jane's Defence Weekly*, *Air Force Magazine*, *Security*, *Survival*, *Navy International*, *Defence and Foreign Affairs* and the *Proceedings of the US Naval Institute*. All the major news magazines and newspapers in the United States were covered, as were those in the UK and many in Western European and Middle Eastern countries.

3. Institutes and Government Departments

Information was also obtained from many research institutes and centres. Among the most useful of these were the Armaments and Disarmament Information Unit at the University of Sussex, England, the Institute for

Defense and Disarmament Studies in Boston, and the Center for Defense Information, the Institute for Policy Studies and the Arms Control Association, all in Washington. Personal contacts with officials in ministries and departments in several countries were also used, but it should be emphasised that this guide relies almost entirely on publicly available information.

Major sources of information often differ in their assessment of the attributes of nuclear weapons systems. This guide was thus necessarily concerned, on occasions, with subjective assessments. Where the author was not completely convinced of the reliability of information, he used phrases such as 'it has been reported that', or 'probably' or, more simply 'perhaps'!

Index

D1196760